F

G

H

I

THOUGHTS FROM A GARDEN SEAT

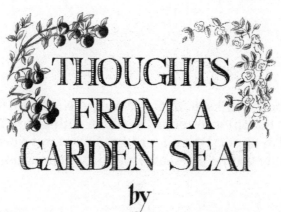

THOUGHTS FROM A GARDEN SEAT

by

Graham Stuart Thomas

Illustrations by Simon Dorrell

JOHN MURRAY
50 Albemarle Street, London

My best thanks go out to Margaret Neal who once again has interpreted my scribble with a sure hand, and to Simon Dorrell for his painstaking work in illustrating the seats from my photographs

G.S.T.

First published in 2000
by John Murray (Publishers) Ltd,
50 Albemarle Street, London W1X 4BD

ISBN 0-7195 5731 3

Typeset in 10/12pt Walbaum Roman by
Servis Filmsetting Limited, Manchester

Printed and bound in Great Britain by
The University Press, Cambridge

This book is offered to those about to walk down
their own garden path

Contents

Introduction   9

            Spring   19
1 Spring in the air   21
2 Planting as in the wild   27
3 Garden seats   34
4 Rhododendrons for spring and winter   37

           Summer   45
5 When summer arrives   47
6 Ornaments for the garden   54
7 Flowers for early summer, and perhaps for
    autumn?   60
8 The later rhododendrons   68
9 Large leaves for creating perspective   74
10 White roses – a review   90

           Autumn   97
11 The joys of autumn   99
12 Paths   108
13 Topiary in all its forms   113
14 The value of lasting foliage   118

           Winter   129
15 Winter work   131
16 Lawns   137

Contents

17 The planting of avenues 140
18 Winter flowers 149

Envoi 155
Location of seats 157

Introduction

'GARDEN' IS ONE of the most loved of English words. It conjures up the beauty and scent of flowers, and sunny days spent tending the borders, the growing of produce, and perhaps a snooze in the sunshine. We are fortunate in Britain to have a great many gardens open regularly to the public, and in them every phase, fashion or style from the last four hundred years is to be found. I am convinced that visiting gardens, wherever possible sitting in them and absorbing them, is the most enjoyable way of learning about gardening.

Although spring and summer are the favoured seasons for garden visiting, even the wintry months have much to offer. For example, it is not until the leaves have fallen that we can appreciate to the full all the wonderful evergreens hardy enough to be grown outside in Britain, unprotected. They give form to the garden landscape and fittingly contrast with the bare branches of other shrubs and trees in the winter sunshine.

Luckily there are gardens open to the public almost daily throughout the winter; some are privately owned, but many belong to the National Trust. If it is quietness you seek, try Lyveden New Bield in Northamptonshire on a sunny winter's day. Probably the only sounds will be the soughing of wind through the trees and the cry of moorhen floating in canals dug centuries ago, with the shell of a unique building in the shape of a cross nearby.

It is a good example of the magic of water, in composition and reflection. Much nearer to London is Claremont at Esher in Surrey, where great work has been done in recent years to re-create the fanciful garden landscape complete with lake, temple and amphitheatre, dating from 1720; apart from the interest of the whole, there are examples of shrubs used at the time. In the grounds of Clumber Park in Nottinghamshire, water and a magnificent chapel combine with many fine trees, both native and exotic, and an avenue of lime or linden trees three miles long to make this one of the most popular 'open spaces' in the country. The soil is poor and sandy; it is thus a good place to see what will grow in what is, apart from its trees, a bleak and barren part of the country – the haunt of Robin Hood. *Rhododendron ponticum* and others flourish, reflected in the lake. To sit on one of the seats and contemplate these reflections as they are rippled by the wind is a solace and refreshment in a busy life.

Away in Northern Ireland, many lovely shrubs grow at Florence Court, but perhaps its most wonderful natural growths are the several fine weeping beeches. These, together with vast trees of rhododendrons, turn a winter visit into a promise to oneself to go again. A splendid place for a winter walk is Studley Royal in Yorkshire, an eighteenth-century landscape garden with formal waters, contemporary buildings and fine trees. The water is fed by a rushing river which farther along its course reflects the ruins of Fountains Abbey.

Stourhead in Wiltshire combines the glory of eighteenth-century inspiration in design with classical buildings. The damming of a stream has resulted in a series of lakes and all the charm that only reflection can give. Apart from being a great period piece, since its inception it has owed much of its interest to exotic species of trees and shrubs. The flare of colour from rhododendrons and azaleas in May and June may offend some purists, but the succession of experiences as one walks round the main lakes or rests on a seat is as enthralling in winter as in summer.

While the gardens so far mentioned owe their attraction mainly to trees, grass and water in the landscape tradition, other gardens open in the winter months are more intimately planted. One specially comes to mind: Polesden Lacey in Surrey. Not only has it a long grass terrace sheltered from cold winds by thickets of yews and trees, but also a small area beyond the main formal gardens where beneath the red-tassled boughs of mighty parrotias are spread carpets of Winter Aconite (*Eranthis hyemalis*), snowdrops, hardy cyclamens and hellebores, guarded by thickets of sweet-scented sarcococcas and many other winter-flowering plants. Polesden is on limy soil, a shallow capping over chalk, but here and there lime-free. At Winkworth Arboretum, also in Surrey, there is a special area given to winter-flowering witch hazels, leading between mahonias, pierises (Lily-of-the-valley bushes) and many more to the area dubbed the summer garden. But we do not necessarily need flowers to entice us to visit Winkworth: there are innumerable shrubs and trees with bark, berry and leaf for our winter delectation, and as the season advances the collection of magnolias will entrance us, sheltered by old stools of cobnuts flinging their catkins and pollen around. It is surprising that such a remarkable collection of trees and shrubs should thrive on the poor sandy banks. Surrey is rich indeed in delights: not far away is Leith Hill and its rhododendron wood, where certain kinds may be in flower as early as February.

Down in the south-west in Devon, on a lime-free hill in an otherwise limy district, is the arboretum at Killerton. Richly planted collections of trees and shrubs make this a place of pilgrimage throughout the year. On the sunny slopes are early and late cyclamens and the pale Pyrenean daffodil, besides early magnolias and rhododendrons. Here, as at Wakehurst Place in Sussex (leased to Kew Gardens and even more richly planted), it is seldom that one could pay a visit without being surprised by out-of-season flowers. There is everything at Wakehurst, not least the splendid walk down the dell, around the bottom lake and back through conifers and birch species to the area specially planted with a selection of shrubs for interest in winter.

With the coming of March and April, gardening once again surges in our blood; primroses and early bulbs beckon us. Of all spring joys, to my mind there is nothing to better the sight of bulbs and little plants naturalised in turf. The drive up to Knightshayes Court in Devon is strewn with thousands of our native Lent Lily (*Narcissus pseudonarcissus*), and the sight of them makes us realise what Wordsworth meant by a 'host of golden daffodils'. The earliest spring bulbs are of course to be found in the south-west, in Cornwall and Devon. In north Devon, high up and in a wet district, lies Arlington Court, where the old trees are hung with many species of moss and green lichen. It is a magical spot in spring, for the areas under the trees are thick with primroses, blushing *Claytonia*, Cuckoo Flower and hardy Wood Sorrel, making a memorable carpet, later to be joined by crimson *Primula japonica*. At Saltram Park, also in Devon, ancient, unnamed cultivars of daffodils and narcissi grow freely along the sides of the old lime avenue. At Mount Stewart in Northern Ireland the daffodils have been segregated as to colour to some extent, to echo the tints of early rhododendrons, which form a widespread company here, and at Rowallane; at Downhill there is a unique assembly of white bluebells and double cuckoo flowers (*Cardamine pratensis* 'Plena') – but do not try to repeat this in your garden, for the plant is a terrible weed in cool moist places.

Something rather special will be found at Lacock Abbey in Wiltshire. Here *Crocus vernus* has spread by seed and with abandon, in purple and paler shades, and I also call to mind the slope by the castle at Sizergh in Cumbria, where early daffodils are followed by orchids and many other meadow flowers. Bluebells are especially in evidence in the oak wood at Winkworth Arboretum in Surrey, also at Emmetts in Kent and in the rides at Blickling Hall, Norfolk. One becomes somewhat satiated with yellow in the early year, from daffodils and forsythias, so that to come on a grouping of white daffodils under white cherries is a pleasant surprise at Cliveden, Berkshire. There are sheets of many kinds of narcissus and daffodils at Sheffield Park and Batemans in Sussex, and at Anglesey Abbey near Cambridge are to be seen not only these same delights but some rare snowdrops and other bulbs.

With the daffodils, and the flowering trees of all sorts that now begin to soften the air with their sweet scent, the rhododendrons start to bloom in earnest (a few are winter-flowering); there is a long succession of them in most Cornish and Devon gardens and elsewhere, ending with the great white *R. auriculatum* in August. Rhododendrons and their allies must have lime-free soil and lots of lime-free humus to ensure their success, and unlike camellias, also for acid soils, they will not put up with drought. While I think it is true to say that an acid soil will be successful with a greater list of plants than a limy one, there is no need to despair if you happen to own a limy plot. There are many great gardens on limy soils, beautiful at all times, with a wide variety of plants. At random I might mention Tintinhull and Barrington Hall in Somerset, Sharpiton in Devon, Polesden Lacey (overlaid in parts by lime-free soil), Mottisfont Abbey in Hampshire, Anglesey Abbey in Cambridgeshire.

As the weeks move on with the passing of all the spring bulbs, the numerous flowering shrubs hold us spellbound with their great glories, headed by the rhododendrons and azaleas. There are the forsythias, red and pink flowering currants (*Ribes*), white viburnums, pale yellow berberises and mahonias, lilacs, species roses mostly in yellow, pink and white, and then the pink and red diervillas, white philadelphuses and all the other garden stalwarts which impart quality and solidity to any border. As their numbers decline with the advancing season – but still with purple, white and pink buddlejas, hydrangeas of all shades, hibiscuses blue, rose and white and cheery ornamental privets to round off the summer – so the hardy herbaceous plants take over the major role of colour-giving. Long the mainstay of high summer and for a hundred years or more grown by themselves, there is now a trend to mix them with the shrubs. This sort of thing was first practised in a general way by Gertrude Jekyll, who deliberately chose for her borders whatever plant or shrub would most enhance her colour schemes, not only by flower colour but by contrast of foliage, green or otherwise tinted. With the early-flowering shrubs comes most of the spring blossom from trees, starting with the greeny-yellow tassels of the Norwegian Maple (*Acer platanoides*), the flowering cherries (*Prunus*) and crab apples (*Malus*), horse chestnuts, magnolias, white Flowering Ash (*Fraxinus ornus*), the pink robinias, and lots more.

There is no lack of colourful summer borders in our gardens. Among other delights to be found at Cliveden are two giant borders, one all fiery tones of red and yellow, the other in subtle subdued shades. There are also very fine borders not devoted to colour schemes. I call to mind Bodnant and Nymans, Blickling, Anglesey

Abbey and Lanhydrock, while at Polesden Lacey the one border, very dry, is given to plants that will thrive in such conditions and also do not require staking, in spite of the wind. Wind is a major factor too in the big border at Killerton; here buddlejas are used to give summer height, and alongside is a series of beds (once used for roses, which never thrived) given to dwarf colourful and foliage plants for year-long interest. It is difficult to think of a garden without a border, whether conventional or not, for such features are often the main summer attraction.

Most roses flower at the same time as the bulk of perennial plants, and special rose gardens are found in many places. There is a unique one tucked away among shrubs at Cliveden, designed with flowing lines, and one in Victorian guise at Shugborough in Staffordshire. Polesden Lacey's ethos is wholly Edwardian, so modern, flashy colours are excluded from the large rose garden. Mottisfont and Nymans have Victorian shrubs and colours. In short, there is no lack of rose gardens, on a wide variety of soils and in every possible situation. Most carry on the beauty of our favourite flower until the autumn; meanwhile, during late summer the half-hardy plants take over, penstemons in many colours, variously tinted argyranthemums, scarlet and purple salvias and the like. Owing to a series of mild winters, we have become venturesome with these and many other plants – like dahlias, the special glory of September (but we have learnt not to leave them in the ground for the winter except in the mildest districts). After its annual summer clipping topiary comes smartly into its own again, but of course topiary pieces and other clipped evergreens punctuate many famous gardens, and hold their own through the year.

There comes a time at the end of September or in early October when the first great autumn fire is to be seen – a tree of *Prunus sargentii*, glowing red before all the other trees turn. Thereafter usually the Japanese maples follow, and then the whole glory of autumn is upon us for October. It is mostly the exotics that turn to brilliant colours; our own natives become yellow or tawny brown, in November. Sheffield Park and Winkworth Arboretum were planted expressly to display autumn colour. At both, lakes reflect the colours, while Sheffield Park has great clumps of silvery Pampas Grass to contrast with the flaming tints. It is a good time, too, for Wakehurst Place and Nymans, and I can think of no moment more rewarding than autumn for a walk round the lake at Stourhead. Bodnant is usually rich in colours too. In the south-west are many gardens of bright leaves, and across the Irish Channel are beautiful Rowallane and Mount Stewart, all worth a long journey. Berried shrubs add to the autumn colour and continue to entrance us after the leaves have fallen. I never think of autumn without calling to mind the smell of bonfires – surely one of the most evocative aromas of the entire year. But no sooner have the leaves fallen than we appreciate afresh the beauties of evergreens – stately conifers, spreading junipers (as at Polesden Lacey), glittering hollies, fragrant Box, and the *Arbutus* or Strawberry Tree so evident at Dunster Castle and Clevedon Court. And so the year goes round; given clear skies and sunshine, there is always something to see – some garden seat to sit on, some garden feature to be enjoyed, dexterously managed for our delectation, surprise and admiration.

Spring

WHEN DOES SPRING begin? The calendars say March 21, but I find that in southern England at least there are many days – sometimes even weeks – during January and February when there is a feeling of spring in the air. 'Little by little the spring begins' sang the poet Swinburne, and how right he was; spells of mild weather alternate with freezing cold that nips the precocious buds. Our native trees and shrubs are wary and do not respond to the touch of spring until well into March; meanwhile we have had a feast of hardy blossom from the many exotic shrubs which grace our gardens.

Though the wintry months may seem long, there is seldom enough time, even with open weather, to complete everything there is to be done in these days. The very weeds know it is the turn of the year, and Bitter Cress and Groundsel flower early and are soon ready even to cast their seeds around. There is never a dull moment; even when all is locked in frost there are jobs to do, such as repairing and sharpening tools, preparing labels and stakes, shaping vine supports and the like. But in the brief pauses when we rest our limbs on the garden seat, we may hear and see a venturesome bumble bee searching for pollen, and quite likely the robin will regale us with his sweet notes. Other birds flit to and fro; as the weeks pass the rooks will start cawing and squabbling in the tree tops, and the missel thrush may be heard 'Flinging his clarion from the Larch'.

March is the month for picking violets, and other little delights abound, the early scillas and crocuses, the Dog's Tooth Violet (*Erythronium*), but above all the daffodils, surely the dominant flower of spring. We are blessed today with varieties that flower from Christmas ('Cedric Morris') through the first few months of the year, ceasing by the middle of May with the great white Pheasant Eye (*Narcissus poeticus recurvus*) and its rare double form, so like the double camellias which flower at the same time and with the same perfection of outline.

CHAPTER ONE

Spring in the air

Spring, the sweet Spring, is the year's pleasant king;
Then blooms each thing, then maids dance in a ring,
Cold doth not sting, the pretty birds do sing -
Cuckoo, jug-jug, pu-wee, to-witta-woo!

Spring, by Thomas Nashe (1567–1601)

THERE IS A saying that, although our weather in Britain may be poor, our climate is good. This paradox arises from the effects of the mild waters of the Gulf Stream which lap our western and northern shores – and indeed also the north-east, as far south as Lincolnshire. But if our climate is good, it is also apt to vary greatly throughout the season and from year to year, making it challenging for gardeners. I have said spring can sometimes be sensed in January or February, but it is also true that winter can start in earnest in these months. An old acquaintance used to claim that 'February sunshine never did nobody no good', which was his way of saying – with a pronounced stutter on 'F-February' – that an early spring (that is, one beginning

before March) was of no use to real gardeners. I think
he was right. Though sunshine is welcome at any time,
as a general rule early warm days often bring disaster
in their train, while a good spell of hard frost and snow
in January or February is beneficial. It helps to kill
certain pests; prevents plants from getting too forward;
and loosens the tilth. By January 4 the lengthening days
become noticeable, and when the thaw comes its pro-
gress is hastened by the sun's ever-growing strength. If
there has been much snow the thaw results in moisture
being released gradually – sinking into the ground
rather than running off. After a late spring growth is
more controlled than in erratic winters of mild days
interspersed with cold.

Does the 'May' in that enigmatic old country saying
'Cast ne'er a clout till May be out' refer to the month, or
the tree (*Crataegus*)? Neither seems especially appropriate. I have known May to flower at any time between
the end of April and the beginning of June, while anyone
tempted by a warm spell early in the month to put away
their winter woollies would do well to heed Dr Buchan.
Dr Alexander Buchan (1827–1907) registered daily tem-
peratures in Scotland over a period of some seventy
years, and found that certain dates brought spells of
cold weather. I learnt many years ago to heed these
dates, even though they are obviously less reliable for
England than for Scotland. The cold spell most to be
feared occurs in early May for three days or so, usually
around the twelfth of the month, and is also known on
the Continent: 'Pancratius, Servatius and Bonifacius,
whose names stand in the calendar against the twelfth,
thirteenth and fourteenth of May, have popularly been
called the [Three] Ice-men in Germany and Austria . . .
They usually bring with them severe frosts at night,
even in the mildest regions of Central Europe, thus
doing incalculable mischief to vegetation.' (From *The*

Natural History of Plants by A.K. von Marilaun, translated by F.W. Oliver, 1895.)

January and February see the need for certain jobs which, if left until later, will delay other works. Whatever the weather, certain weeds will grow, and no time should be lost in removing them. Country lanes and pieces of neglected ground show nature hard at work, with Cuckoo Pint or Lords and Ladies and Cow Parsley among the first natives to herald the burgeoning year. Higher up the dusky leaves of the Elder are growing, and by the end of February the twigs of Hawthorn will be throwing a film of bright green over hedge and copse. Some of us may remember the tiny leaves of the Elm, but I fear it will be some decades before its roots have thrown off the lethal effects of the elm disease, its fungus and its beetles.

It is my idea that Spring does not really make itself felt until the March winds are with us. Even March can be bitterly cold, but there is something in the movement of the air and the slowly increasing strength of the sun which gives us confidence. Many bulbs, such as snowdrops and aconites, will have come and gone by early March, together with the several delectable shrubs detailed in the last section of this book. A Maple, one of the very earliest trees to flower, will catch our eyes – *Acer opalus*, which decorates its leafless branches with tassels of bright greeny-yellow – echoed a fortnight later by the similarly prolific Norwegian Maple, *A. platanoides*. Bunches of crimson stamens will be lighting up the tiered branches of *Parrotia persica* or Iron Wood, a very large shrub or tree which, like the two maples, is too big for the average garden. *Parrotia* excels in autumn colour too, and this is what is so wonderful about our gardens today: there is no closed season unless we are frozen hard. In *Cuttings from my Garden*

Notebooks I made November the beginning of the garden year, by virtue of the *Mahonia* hybrids which begin to flower then, and the clearing away of deciduous leaves. But March is just as good a start.

A few perennials are eager to burst into bloom before all others, among them the common Primrose and the Lungwort. In older clumps in corners protected by shrubs or walls the Primrose may be counted on to brave the weather and produce odd blooms early in the New Year, as may the Lungwort (*Pulmonaria*) – known as 'Spotted Dog' or 'Soldiers and Sailors' from, respectively, the white-spotted bristly leaves and the flowers which ring the changes on red and blue. The characteristic both plants have in common is that of seeding themselves everywhere except in the driest of conditions. I should never begrudge its space to a primrose of any colour, for its abundant bloom, but pulmonarias, at their best in March, are apt to choose a spot next to some choice small plant, and by the time May is with us will have produced an overwhelming tuft of handsome but coarse leaves. They are so prolific that it is wise to remove all flowering shoots before they seed, and also to dig up unwanted seedlings before they get too large. It is necessary to dig out all the thong-like roots, for any left behind will sprout in a few weeks. Even so, I should not wish my garden to be totally without them.

Pulmonaria picta (which used to be called *P. saccharata*) has flowers of pinky-red or blue. One which occurred here with flowers of bright coral-pink and extra-spotted leaves I named 'Leopard', and it is found in several lists. Colours vary from pink to blue, according to age and parentage. At one time *P. officinalis* with distinct stalks to its leaves could be distinguished from *P. picta*, which has larger leaves, but they are much hybridised in gardens today. Most forms with particularly good leaves owe their origin to the latter species; some are almost wholly grey throughout the season, and very handsome they are. Among the selected forms I grow are the fine blue 'Bertram Anderson', the appealing 'Sissinghurst White' and the dainty smaller *P. officinalis* 'Cambridge Blue'. A little later to flower are the true blue *P. azurea* and *P. mollis*, which seldom increase by seeding. The former, with bristly leaves, is a very showy plant, echoed by the latter, with broad leaves quite velvety to the touch. Their glorious blue flowers come just at the right time for underplanting forsythias. We seldom see *Physochlaina orientalis*, which bears a superficial resemblance to the pulmonarias of the Borage family, but is grouped with the potato in Solanaceae. Its pretty pale blue flowers are among the earliest of the year's herbaceous perennials.

There is not much time to sit and look at the joys of spring if you have not been busy in February, when all those *Clematis* varieties which flower on the young wood – that is, almost all those which flower from July onwards – should have been cut down. If your garden is alive with snails, I should not cut them down below one foot, which will at least put the snails to some trouble to get at the succulent young shoots in April! Any shrubs still sporting berries that have survived through the winter can be left for later pruning, but it is time to cut down or back shrubs grown solely for the beauty of their coloured bark, such as varieties of Dogwood (*Cornus alba*) and certain willows (*Salix*). The best colour is revealed on new wood, but I am averse to too-severe cutting. If you take out half only of the previous year's growth and shorten the rest, you will still have a shrub to enjoy.

Weeding is an occupation to which we must give our best endeavours, in order to defeat the little troubles while they are still young. I am convinced that the most effective way of dealing with weeds is to go for one species at a time, and against trying to get a garden completely free of them at one fell swoop, unless it is very small. I think it much better to set about those weeds which are on the point of flowering and setting seeds. Thus I would go round the garden early in the year and get rid of all the groundsels and Hairy Bitter Cress first; a week or two later, I would pull up all the Shepherd's Purse and dig up the celandines. Keep a watch through the year for successive crops of weeds and destroy them before they seed. In summer the little *Epilobium* or willow herbs will be a nuisance, but fortunately their tiny pink flowers catch the eye just in time, before seeding starts.

CHAPTER TWO

Planting as in the wild

THERE CAN BE few mortals who are not moved by the appearance of spring-flowering bulbs in short grass, perhaps under deciduous trees. The area given to such a planting is not material – the great thing is the emergence of new growth and spring flowers. It entails no gardening, in the sense of the digging and planting of borders. But spring is immediately apparent, and no matter how small the area we sense the swing of the year. Even if the ground is poor and rooty spring–flowering bulbs will usually thrive, oblivious of summer shade. It should not be a neatly prescribed area, cut off from the normal borders of the garden, but should merge into them through low shrubs, ferns, Solomon's Seal (*Polygonatum*) and other things – these for shady areas: a different selection would be needed for a sunny site.

When setting out to devote an area, whether small or large, to this most delightsome of plantings there are a few 'don'ts' to be remembered. Starting from scratch, it is absolutely vital that there shall be no deep-rooted perennial weeds in the area, as it will be impossible to get rid of them after bulbs have been planted. One or even two full growing seasons will be well spent watching for and eradicating aliens, to make quite sure that only small annual weeds are present.

To me the best way of planting such an area with spring bulbs is to plant the purchased stock temporarily, in rows in a spare piece of well dug and fertile ground. Of these little bulbs, the cheapest to buy will usually be well-tried kinds which increase freely, which is what we want; the more expensive will usually be newer or slow of increase. (Whatever you do, avoid the little onion *Allium triquetrum*; cheap to buy, it is a too-prolific spreader by bulb and seed.) It is good to see how they multiply in the course of a couple of years in a nursery bed, thus keeping expenditure to the minimum. The delay will in addition fix in our minds the colours and heights of the bulbs, so that an intelligent distribution can be arranged at planting time. The intervening months can be used imagining where the most important drifts of bulbs should be planted – where we need the major groups, where the scattered outliers, supposing the major groups to have spread by seed into little extra colonies. It is attention to details like this that can make or mar our planting.

When you have decided on the area and effectively removed the perennial weeds by good cultivation – and kept the hoe going for the destruction of little weeds and annual grasses – it is time to start planting. There is no time so good for moving bulbs from nursery rows into new permanent quarters as immediately after flowering. It does the bulbs no harm; moreover, the foliage indicates where and what you have planted – so different from planting dry bulbs in autumn, when they become at once invisible. With the foliage left on in spring you can intermingle the drifts and use your artistry to imitate nature's own efforts, except that hers take many years whereas you are attempting the job in a couple of seasons.

The first real display is given by that cheapest and most prolific spreader, *Crocus tomasinianus*, whose little cups of deep lilac will gladden the heart some cold February day, and on into March. They are shortly followed by another good spreader, *C. etruscus*, rather deeper in colour and prettily striped without. The common Snowdrop, *Galanthus nivalis*, will grow as a rule in thin grass but favours a rather stiff limy soil; it seeds itself, whereas the double form needs division except where it is extra prolific.

We will want to include all sorts of delectable spring bulbs – crocuses, snowdrops, chionodoxas, scillas, erythroniums – but it is the daffodils that walk away with the prize; and for a true semblance of the wild it is the miniature narcissi and daffodils, species and the many hybrids raised by Alec Gray and others, that are most desirable. Not for our scheme are the vulgar great grandiflora daffodils so beloved by municipal planters and florists. They do not spread by seed, but merely remain in clumps, as planted. It is the scale that is wrong. In some great gardens you may see several acres given over to large-flowered daffodils and narcissi, and here they are in scale; the only disadvantage is that in these sorts the doubles and singles, trumpets and cups, in yellow and white and orange (which make up what are known as 'naturalising mixtures'), are usually all over in a month or so, or even less.

One of the first daffodils to flower, giving me almost more delight than all others put together, is our native Lent Lily, *Narcissus pseudonarcissus*, only about 6 inches high. There is something particularly winsome about its slightly nodding blooms, its forward-pointing perianth petals of paler colour than the yellow trumpet. It is of course one of those few species that have given rise to the whole gamut of garden daffodils. A prolific spreader by seed, it thus achieves for us the natural scattering of outlying bulbs around the area planted; whole fields of it may be seen in western counties, and occasionally in the east. Quite different is the wild Welsh daffodil, *N. obvallaris*, or Leek, as it is called. In this the foliage is taller, of a bluer green, and the flowers are borne well aloft, in piercing bright yellow with a greenish or sulphur tint. It has never sown itself in my garden, but I cannot imagine this would be true in the Welsh valleys; on the other hand, the bulbs increase freely. Another noted early flowerer, for moist soil, is *N. cyclamineus*, whose perianth segments are swept back as its name suggests; those and the trumpet together bear some resemblance to a Christmas cracker. Rather later, also enjoying damp ground, is the Hoop Petticoat Daffodil, *N. bulbocodium*. While the trumpet opens wide, as its name indicates, its petals are reduced to a narrow pointed star. Both species increase freely by seed and may be seen in their thousands in the early year at Wisley and the Savill Garden.

It is difficult to recommend only a few of the miniature hybrid daffodils – there are so many candidates. A random selection of favourites, freely increasing though seldom by seed, is headed by the early 'February Gold', closely followed by 'March Sunshine' and 'Little Witch', 'Larkelly' and 'Beryl'. They are all charmers and increase well. I should not want to exclude the old 'Barrii Conspicuus', a cool yellow with tiny orange cup. This has always delighted me because of its scent, no doubt inherited from the early white Pheasant Eye, one of the best of which is 'Actaea'. With it flowers the beautiful white 'Thalia', with somewhat recurved perianth and rounded cup inherited from *N. triandrus*. Last but not least and flowering well into May is the late Pheasant Eye, *N. poeticus recurvus*, of great beauty and delicious scent. It increases freely, but like all these needs lifting and dividing from time to time.

One particularly valuable variety is 'Rockery White', because it is virtually the first to flower of those with white perianth segments, most of which derive from later-flowering species such as *N. poeticus* and *N. triandrus*. In the welter of hybrids and selected forms it is difficult to find any to be cast out – all are beautiful excepting double forms, though here I must plead for the inclusion of *N. moschatus* 'Plenus' (*N. cernuus* 'Plenus'), whose modest cream trumpets are filled with small segments. With a careful selection we can have these little bulbs in flower for six or eight weeks, ending with the sweetly scented hybrids of *N. triandrus* and *N. poeticus*. One of my latest-flowering treasures, extending into May in some years, is 'Tittle Tattle', with dainty small yellow blooms and a pronounced fragrance.

What are we to do about bluebells? In any ordinary soil the Spanish Bluebell (*Hyacinthoides hispanica*) will seed itself with abandon; likewise, in good moist soil, our native Bluebell, *Hyacinthoides non-scripta*, which is slightly darker and later, and with arching spikes. Once allowed in, these will both seed themselves so prolifically as to crowd out the smaller bulbs. I recommend banishment, lovely though they are.

With the very earliest of daffodils in March comes *Scilla bifolia* in pure blue; it first appears in the variety 'Praecox' and is quickly followed by the type species; these seed themselves freely. There is quite a range of beauty from the Glory of the Snow (*Chionodoxa*) – *C. forbesii* (*C. lucilliae* of gardens) in light blue; its varieties 'Pink Giant' and 'Rosea' in light pink; also the species *C. sardensis* in vivid rich blue, with less of the white centre displayed by the others. All of these spread freely by seeds, whereas the intergeneric hybrid × *Chionoscilla allenii* – a good cobalt blue – does not, and needs division for its increase. But the prince of all these spring blues is undoubtedly *Scilla siberica*, especially its form 'Spring Beauty', a glorious rich blue. And each bulb sends up several stems, each stem bearing several blooms – a peer without price, in beauty for three weeks or more.

Once all the bulbs are planted, it is important not to relax. If the larger ones are at a suitable depth of 4 to 6 inches, you can continue to hoe during the summer, getting ready for sowing the grass in August or early September. This is a movable operation, depending on whether rain has fallen and on the nature of the ground. Make sure you obtain only fine lawn grasses in the seed mixture. Often some coarse native grasses will invade the plot; these should be removed piecemeal before they become too large. In after years, the first mowing will be done about June 15, when the bulbs are over or their foliage can be cut away with impunity. Further mowing will be needed later in the year, according to the rainfall, and short grass will ensure that autumn leaves can be raked off easily.

So far it has been a fairly simple job. It is when your enthusiasm increases and you start planting such things as aconites (*Eranthis*) and cyclamens, which cannot be hoed over, that the difficulties usually start – compounded if you hanker after autumn-flowering bulbs, which upset the mowing programme. Fortunately, today's spin-trim and other rotary mowers will come to your aid in between the planted areas: if only they were not so anti-social because of the noise they make. I have a weakness for colchicums, the Naked Ladies whose crocus-like goblets enchant us in September. There are autumn-flowering crocuses and snowdrops too, but these had better be omitted until you have fully grasped the expertise that will be needed to cope with such disparate plants.

Devoting a separate area to spring bulbs means that we can forget their untidy leaves once the display of early blossom is past, and revel in our well-groomed beds and borders. But in the many gardens too small to include a sufficient area of rough grass, one must look around for other places to grow them. One method is to plant clumps in the mixed border – but what then of those fading, bedraggled leaves? The best solution I think is to plant the groups around the edges of stalwart, larger plants which will provide smothering greenery soon after the flowers of the bulbs are over. Such things as hostas come to mind, fuchsias, hardy agapanthus hybrids, peonies, and the like – also deciduous shrubs.

There are, however, gardeners who do not wish for trim beds and borders and would love to see all their plants growing with abandon in rough grass, something like a mediaeval *millefleurs* tapestry. Imagine clumps of peonies growing wild, as it were, followed by agapanthuses, both for sunny situations, or in shade great clumps of hostas, *Smilacina*, and rheums for big schemes, with rodgersias for moist ground. And in my mind's eye there is an area devoted to the various Japanese anemones. Few plants can give so prolonged and gracious a display as these stalwart perennials and, considering their errant and potentially troublesome prolificity, I can think of no way of growing and appreciating their beauty with so little trouble. Clumps of ornamental grasses would not only complete the picture but also supply just that contrast of foliage needed. And at their feet, supplementing their colours, would be clumps of colchicums, in rosy lilac and white.

From a small patch to be devoted to spring bulbs we have journeyed through the year using the same plot for a semi-natural distribution of meadow plants. It only remains for you to carry it out. It is not as easy as it sounds, but well worth the attempt.

CHAPTER THREE

Garden seats

MOST OF US are used to seeing seats in gardens placed with much less thought than is given to their counterparts indoors; and yet, we are considering the principal piece of furniture of the garden. A seat should rightly be given an important position. It can grace a terrace, finish a vista, suitably interrupt a too-long border, or be placed informally just where there is a good view. There are many different but traditional shapes for garden seats. The most comfortable are those with 'dished' – that is, slightly concave – rather than uncompromisingly flat seats, which are uncomfortable and need cushions for more than the briefest stay. The ultimate in elegance is, I suppose, the Lutyens bench and its derivatives; yet Lutyens did not design his bench with dished seating. In windy gardens, even a dense evergreen hedge will prove to be of little use against draughts; what is needed here is a seat with a solid wooden back. This is a matter of priority in making an initial choice – there is nothing so disastrous as a draughty back: the seat doesn't matter so much. And there must be, and usually are, rests for the arms.

There is an open choice as to shape and finish, to suit personal taste and the dictates of the garden and position. While softwood can be painted to any colour, oak and some tropical woods which do not take kindly to paint may be stained, or left in their natural state. A well-painted seat will not attract the lichens and mosses which are apt to settle on natural wood and need to be brushed off occasionally. On no account should a wire brush be used, and any brushing should be across the grain; brushing along the grain will tend to deepen it, making it more welcoming to mossy growths.

The colour of a seat should reflect the owner's tastes and be sympathetic to its surroundings, but I would make one recommendation: only if the seat is of good design should it be given a light colour. Anything commonplace should be painted to melt into the background: for a nondescript piece of furniture a nondescript colour is I think the best, somewhere between green and brown, black or grey. Like white (a glaring horror in full sunlight), black is unsympathetic on wood; green, if chosen, should not war with natural greenery. The architect Charles Wade used at Snowshill Manor in Gloucestershire a decidedly greenish blue, known as Wade Blue, and by scraping away successive layers of paint on doors and woodwork at Hidcote we found that much the same tint had been chosen by Lawrence Johnston. Brown is perhaps too autumnal for a seat which is mainly for the summer months. Sometimes, too, one must bear in mind what tint the paint may develop on fading; there is much to be learnt. It is wise to put wooden seats under cover for the winter, and a dry shed or glasshouse provides both safe storage and a place for winter work on repairs or painting.

Seats of metal, if properly coated with paint, can stand out in all weathers. They may be old and heavy, of cast iron, or modern, of light-weight alloy. The one thing to guard against is the rust that starts to accumulate at joints in cast iron. My own preference for metal seats is to avoid all colours except white, black, and indeterminate greys. Much depends on the colour of the background and the design of the seat. Something simple in strap iron is perhaps best in black or darkest grey, while an involved lacy design will show to advantage against a contrasting background, although staring white should be avoided; an off-white or pale grey will enhance an intricate design set against a dark hedge, or give a light-hearted effect among silvery foliage. I have seen a violet-blue tint used with great effect against a yew hedge, and a dark purple in a garden devoted mainly to white flowers. Many enthusiasts dare not trust their own likes and dislikes, and fall back on the thought that black or white will please most people. It is a defeatist attitude. Artistry in the selection of colours for seats can give the garden a stamp of its own and enhance both the planting and the background. But all this must go hand in hand with the quality of the design.

There remain the seats of stone found in old, large gardens. Of course they need no paint, only a brush off now and again, but few of us can afford them and, while they may well provide a strong architectural feature, they are cold and unsympathetic to the human frame. More than any others, they need cushions.

A garden seat should be a perfect, peaceful refuge from which to observe the changing seasons. If you are *making* a seat, of wood, metal or stone, be sure to provide a dished bench, and a slightly sloping rear upright at an angle which supports the back. Then you will be able to enjoy sitting on it as soon as the first warm days arrive, revelling in the spring flowers as they come out, and so on as the year progresses. This is one of the great pleasures of life.

CHAPTER FOUR

Rhododendrons for spring and winter

B EING BROUGHT UP, as I was, on the sticky, limy soil of
Cambridge was not the best introduction to rhododendrons. Only in the University Botanic Garden were
they to be seen, in beds prepared deeply with peat, and
there they grew only half-heartedly. The peat in those
days was what was called 'orchid' peat – square lumps
of fibrous material threaded through with roots of
bracken.

There is no doubt that rhododendrons, coupled with
the azaleas which are today included in the genus, are
a study on their own. Many enthusiastic gardeners on
lime-free soil in the damper areas find them enough,
almost, to feed their gardening appetites to the exclu-
sion of other plants. This is not altogether surprising,
since rhododendrons flower at any time between
November and August and range in height from a few
inches to twenty or more feet – bald facts which may
surprise the average gardener who thinks of these
plants as May and June splendour of average size. In
colour they embrace the whole spectrum except true
blue. Then there are the leaves, in length from half an

inch to two feet, of every tint of green, some rough, some smooth. Some of the smaller species have short-stalked flowers which may be likened to violas, others are borne in small starry heads; yet others may be said to imitate lilies in their regal beauty.

Remove rhododendrons from many of our great gardens, and a disappointing gap would occur in spring and early summer. They make such a splash of colour, scarcely equalled and certainly not surpassed by any other genus, that it might be thought that a garden could not be successful without them. Yet they have some strict cultural requirements, apart from a lime-free soil: they are thirsty plants (unlike camellias), and when peaty soil gets dry it takes a lot of moistening. Again, spring frosts are anathema to them, and there is usually only one crop of flower to be spoiled. Except for a few they do not need full sunshine, but prefer broken shade. They require some form of humus added to the soil, both as an ingredient and as a mulch, and do not take kindly to ground-cover plants, which rob them of moisture. And the soil in general needs to be of a friable nature and not clay. Subject to these admonishments, they are easy to grow, except on windy sites where the rocking of the plants will result in a loosening of the root-ball.

Since most gardens of today are too small for them, I will deal with the real giants of the race later. For the winter months there is a group of shrubs of medium size. Soon after Christmas appear *R. dauricum*, of which a noted form is 'Midwinter', and *R. mucronulatum*. These two species carry flowers of deep rosy lilac, but of the latter there are two forms worth bearing in mind, the pure white 'Album' and 'Winter Brightness'. There is also, a little later, the hybrid 'Praecox', a shade paler lilac but a fine bushy shrub. This in turn is followed by pale pink 'Cilpinense' and also 'Christmas Cheer', which in my garden seldom flowers before early March; alone of the above it is of a normal big, bushy growth. The yellow *R. lutescens* with its coppery young foliage, the creamy, effective 'Bo Peep' and 'Yellow Hammer' follow soon; the last usually gives a crop of flowers in November as well. *Rhododendron leucaspis* is creamy white with chocolate-coloured anthers and there is also the beautiful *R. moupinense* in white or clear pink.

By April in Surrey one may expect several good tough lavender-blue species and hybrids of lowly stature, with small flowers freely borne, such as *R. impeditum*, *R. hippophaeoides* (of which the best form is known as 'Sunningdale' or 'Haba Shan'), *R. scintillans* (*R. polycladum* Group) and *R. russatum* in violet. Taller hybrids are 'Blue Tit', 'Blue Diamond' and 'Blue Bird'; the last is noted for its pretty contrast of yellowish young foliage. In fact, these all benefit from the contrast of yellow, and fortunately *R. rupicola* var. *chryseum* supplies it; the delectable 'Logan Damaris' also excels in clear good yellow, but is much larger in growth and flower. A small lilac-pink is 'Pink Drift'.

It is at about this time, too, in late April or early May, that certain azaleas come into flower. One of the first is the pretty *R. vaseyi* in pale pink with long recurving stamens, and the exquisite *R. schlippenbachii*. Both flower from the bare branches. The earliest of the Mollis Group of azaleas will also start to open. Compared with other azaleas the Mollis Group always seems to me a little brash, but who on a cold May day can resist the warmth of 'Koster's Brilliant Red'? It is not really red, but a warm, flaming orange-red with coral overtones. 'Spek's Brilliant' and 'Mrs Peter Koster' are other similarly vibrant hues, and there are good soft yellows such as 'Christopher Wren'. 'Norma' is a noted double in rose-red.

If you live in very mild areas – as at Trengwainton, in

farthest Cornwall – you can flood your garden in spring
with a succession of the tender, scented rhododendrons,
such as the well-known conservatory plant 'Fragrant-
issimum'; this leads in general recognition a group of
exquisite, mainly white kinds of lily-like perfection,
gloriously scented. 'White Wings' and 'Tyermannii' are
noted contributors.

One of the best-known species is *R. yunnanense*, of
large size but regularly covered with small flowers of
various tones of creamy-white or blush or mauve, with
chestnut markings in the throat. Its near relative *R.
pseudoianthinum* is a useful colour to add as a blender,
a rich wine-purple. Always worth including in any collection is *R. racemosum*, its name referring to the habit
this plant has of making long shoots, which in the following spring are studded along their length with clear
pink small flowers. It is hardy and reliable.

As April turns into May, the genus comes well into its
own. Of the range of shrubs available we might start with
some tinies, such as *R. campylogynum* and its even
smaller variety *myrtilloides*, a mere mat of green leaves
above which are held bell-like blooms on slender stalks
in tones of port wine, but covered with a grey-white
bloom. Both of these and the next are suited to ledges in
a cool moist rock garden, or a peat garden. Those of the
Saluenense Series are also small-leafed, and hold their
viola-like flowers well aloft. The smallest is perhaps *R.
uniflorum*; *R. pemakoense* and *R. calostrotum* may
ascend to a foot. The last has good greyish foliage which
contrasts well with the best claret-red form, 'Harry
White', also known as 'Gigha'. Still of lowly growth are *R.
forrestii repens* and its forms and hybrids, including
'Lava Flow'; their flowers are comparatively large, and
of blazing red. These are all lowly plants, just right for a
cool slope on the rock garden, or in front of larger shrubs.

My mention of *R. calostrotum* and its cool greeny-grey

foliage calls mind that with May upon us the season's young foliage is much to the fore, and rhododendrons have more to offer than just flowers: *R. chameunum*, Award of Merit form, previously known as *R. saluenense*, has very dark, coppery foliage. I noticed earlier the remarkable copper beech colouring of the young leaves of *R. lutescens*; the foliage of 'Elizabeth Lockhart' strikes one of the deepest notes in the garden and lasts into late summer. But glaucous foliage is to be found too, in species such as *R. cinnabarinum* and its near relatives *R. concatenans* and *R. xanthocodon*. While the first is available in several flower tints, including orange and port-wine colour, the last two are usually of a rich Chinese yellow; all have pretty dangling bells. Their remarkable leaves led to their being used in the Spanish garden at Mount Stewart in Northern Ireland, where the focal tints were from glaucous *Hosta sieboldiana* and *Kniphofia caulescens* and plants with pale yellow and wine-red flowers, bolstered by the magnificent tree peony 'Souvenir de Maxime Cornu'.

But this is only to touch on the subject of leaf-colour in rhododendrons, and one must also bear in mind a few other very remarkable plants. One is the lowly *R. lepidostylum*, whose leaves, small and narrow, are of a pale turquoise tint ringed with pale hairs; the branches of pale yellow flowers are a pleasant soft complement. The ultimate is the variant of *R. campanulatum* known as 'Hooker's form', *R.c. aeruginosum*. If we translate this term as 'verdigris' we shall have an idea of the startling blue shade of the young leaves. It is worth a day's journey to see this plant at its best. An early flowerer which will achieve some 9 feet in time, *R. niveum* is a unique species with a colour scheme less surprising but all its own, silvery leaves and blooms in tight trusses of cool lilac. I like it especially when underplanted with white daffodils.

It is at this early mid season that the giants mostly flower. Anyone with the space required in the right soft climate can hardly resist planting *R. sinogrande,* whose leaves are the largest of their kind. Rather smaller is *R. falconeri,* which will tolerate harsher conditions. Its creamy flowers, like those of *R. sinogrande,* are held in imposing trusses, but it has lesser leaves of khaki green, brown beneath. The hardiest of the group is *R. rex ficto- lacteum* and its sister *R. rex* with very dark foliage, brown beneath, which shows up the creamy flowers well. I have seen this giving a good account of itself exposed to all the cold north winds in Northumberland, while at Mount Stewart in Northern Ireland *R. maca- beanum* thrives on a rather dry bank (but Mount Stewart has a fairly high rainfall), its great leaves setting off the trusses of cool yellow bells.

In early May other azaleas apart from the early Mollis varieties already mentioned begin to make themselves felt. There are the compact little bushes of the very earliest of the semi-evergreen Kurume or Japanese azaleas. 'Kure no Yuki' is a beautiful pure white, but the variety of tints available includes true red ('Hinodegire'), clear pink ('Hino mayo') and shades of puce and mauve. The spectrum is so wide in these plants that they require the utmost forethought in their placing to avoid destructive colour clashes. I remember as a schoolboy seeing a poor, wizened, half-dead bush with two pink flowers on a nurseryman's rubbish heap. I asked if I could have it, and was overjoyed when in subsequent years, cosseted in peat at a shilling per peck, it began to flourish and flower freely. It turned out to be 'Hino mayo', the yardstick against which all other Kurumes should be measured, the most willing and free-flower- ing of all; unfortunately, none of them have fragrance. They are all small-flowered, but make up for this in the way they crowd their branches with flowers, making a dominating mass. No doubt way back in their parentage is the vigorous *R.* 'Amoenum', whose tabular growths are so spectacular when covered with hundreds of tiny flowers of rich crimson-purple. The variety 'Coccineum' is a brighter red, but apt to revert to the original colour.

While the Kurume azaleas are small-flowered and mainly compact and semi-dwarf, during this century several strains have grown up of equal floriferousness but rather larger in growth and flower, descended mainly from *R. malvaticum* and *R. kaempferi*. This parentage will prepare us for strange mixtures of colours from soft mauve to coral and brick red. Those of the latter tint are often very late-flowering, in fact 'Mikado' and 'Naomi' are among the latest-flowering of azaleas. 'John Cairns' is earlier, and 'Rosebud' is a dainty double pink of low growth.

I have a special weakness for the section known as the Ghent azaleas, partly due to their long curving stamens and comparatively small flowers. Among the most sought-after is 'Altaclerense', raised at Highclere, a splendid grower in rich yellow. One of the latest to flower is 'Bouquet de Flore', in a pleasing blend of pink and soft yellow; 'Nancy Waterer' is wholly yellow. I suppose the most popular are the almost indistinguishable 'Gloria Mundi' and 'Coccineum Speciosum', which I think just has the edge on 'Coccineum Major'. Their fierce orange-red needs the whole landscape to itself. The hybridising which started at Knap Hill Nursery in the middle of the nineteenth century with the aim of improving the Ghent azaleas was carried on at Exbury in Hampshire, where from the 1920s and 30s a race of large-flowered and very splendid plants occurred. Who wanting brilliance in their garden could resist the butter-yellow 'Marion Merriman', white 'Oxydol' and pink 'Strawberry Ice', and 'Hotspur' in orange-vermilion?

Summer

THE COMING OF summer can be as hesitant as spring's arrival. Though the evenings lengthen in June it is often too cool to sit out, and in fact it is often something of a shock to realise that the longest day – June 21, Midsummer Day – has passed without our feeling too hot; on the other hand, 'flaming June' just as often beguiles us into thinking that summer has really arrived. But warm nights seldom come before July, so that to me June is part of spring, while summer embraces July and August.

Summer is the time to enjoy all the garden fragrances, not only those of the most scented plants but also the smell of freshly mown grass and the grateful aroma of parched soil refreshed by a shower. Summer evenings are special times for sitting on a garden seat in contemplation – protected by insect repellant – and pondering on the day's work past and all there is still to do: for a gardener, as for a housewife, there are always jobs to do. One of my most repetitive tasks is to pull up the several varieties of willow herbs (*Epilobium*) directly they open their little pink flowers. And I am sometimes (not *often*) horrified to see a Sow-thistle on the point of seeding!

Summer is the time to consider whether we have all the garden joys in their best places – best for successful cultivation, and for associating one with another. It so happens that the various spring flowers each come with a rush and are soon over, whereas many summer flowers are with us for several weeks – hence the need for careful colour scheming, particularly of perennial plants and the few shrubs that are still to flower, the purple and pink buddlejas, white hoherias and hydrangeas, and fuchsias of many tints that, with potentillas and the heathers, will see us through till September. As for roses, they are with us all the summer from June onwards, and their colours invite us to grow them combined with other plants, not just in beds on their own.

Late summer is the season for the great garden spiders, variously tinted, often with a white cross on their backs. Some are large enough to tackle a wasp or a bee enmeshed in their superlative webs, while at the approach of September the ungainly daddy-long-legs run a poor chance of getting free before they are pounced upon and rapidly wrapped in silken threads. The garden seat is a great spot from which to observe the clever making of these symmetrical webs, but they are woven at break of day and an early – a very early – breakfast would have to be ordered. Except for the white ones, butterflies are often not seen much in my district until late August and September, apart from the earlier feast that the buddlejas provide. It is a remarkable fact that the most common and colourful species, the peacocks, tortoiseshells and commas, in their mainly brown and reddish colouring, seem particularly devoted to flowers of pink, mauve and lilac tints – not a combination which would be considered good taste in gardening!

CHAPTER FIVE

When summer arrives

THIS BLISSFUL STATE for which we all long is not without its disadvantages. It is a true saying that no blessing is unalloyed – perhaps the Cold Spell which Dr Buchan observed to occur with some regularity at the junction of June and July will cause us to put on our winter clouts yet again; alternatively, a heat-wave may beset us and cause resort to the hose and sprinklers.

Then there is grooming to be done – a job which is with us throughout the growing season: dead-heading, and removal of faded leaves. For the fullest enjoyment of a garden there should be no sign of fading or deterioration. In well nurtured ground, this cutting-back of flower stems may encourage many plants to put forth new flowers, while with subjects such as irises the aim is to improve their appearance. Apart from *Iris pallida dalmatica*, whose very grey foliage remains in beauty till the autumn, I think most of the usual Bearded irises are more presentable in the late summer garden if the foliage is reduced. By mid August most of their leaves have begun to look untidy and flop around, losing the handsome vertical line which they give in the early year.

There is one job which, if left undone, can mar the best effect of well-stocked borders, and that is grass-mowing. One enterprising gardener I know derives great satisfaction from always mowing along the stripes the same way, thus accentuating the 'pile'. While it has a salutary effect, it is not a practice I should recommend. There is no doubt that a well-cut lawn gives that polished touch to a garden, but sometimes visitors come at the wrong moment! It is my opinion that it is even more important to attend to the edges than the mowing: slightly shaggy grass can be forgiven so long as the edges are trim.

It is a wonderful thought that just when humans are enjoying the fragrance and colour of the summer weather, the birds are benefiting from the multitudes of insects to feed their young. Full summer, though short, has an exuberance not belonging to any other time, while the long days enable plants to set and ripen their seeds, ready for next year. Yet much as I dislike the bitter cold of winter, I should not want to live in a climate of perpetual summer. The contrast of the changing seasons is one of the great delights of living in a Temperate climate. And for us gardeners, every season brings fresh joys.

Now, in early July, with the fragrant lilacs long past, it is the season of roses, of the Mock Orange or *Philadelphus* with its profuse white flowers and delicious scent, and of the heavily fragrant Linden or lime trees. These, together with fields of beans and red clover, have one thing in common: they are not 'fast of their smells', as Sir Francis Bacon put it; their fragrance is 'free on the air'. There is much in this matter not at once apparent. Some roses are fast of their smells – you have to pick a bloom and sniff it – whereas others cast their fragrance freely. My small researches have led me as far as the fact that rose species belonging to the Musk

Section (botanically, those of the Synstylae) – *Rosa brunonii*, *R. mulliganii*, *R. multiflora* and their relatives –
produce their fragrance in their stamens, not in their
petals as in other species, and this is also true of
Philadelphus species. It is easy to detect: simply pull
the petals off a flower, and if the fragrance is in the
stamens you will find it remains. Whether this is the
governing factor in the freedom of fragrance, I cannot
say; summer rushes by so quickly that all one's reso-
lutions to do a little detective work get put aside. It
would be interesting to know, for instance, whether this
same phenomenon is also found in *Malus* 'Profusion'
and *Rhododendron* 'Angelo', and in the usual border
phloxes, all of which are very free of their scent.

Returning to the Synstylae roses, I expect that many
modern varieties like 'Fragrant Cloud' owe their wonderful free scent to a Synstylae species – such as *R. moschata*, *R. multiflora* or *R. phoenicea* – way back in their
parentage. This freedom of fragrance is nullified by dry
east winds but fostered and enhanced by the warm soft
air of summer, particularly after rain, which is when the
Sweet Briar (*R. eglanteria*) gives forth its benison from
its leaves, as do the lavenders and many other herbs,
and the great Gum Cistus, *C. ladanifer*, and its hardy
hybrid *C.* × *cyprius*. There is no doubt that with due
practice, the nose can be as great an asset in the garden
as the eye is.

Perhaps this is the place to consider as well the shrubs
and plants which cast their fragrance freely on the air at
other times of the year. Lovely though it may be to bury
one's nose in a handful of pinks or a bunch of violets, as
a gardener I want to be greeted by scents as I walk
around. Early in the year there is nothing to touch the
Witch Hazel or *Hamamelis mollis*, of which I prefer
the brighter yellow of the hybrid 'Pallida'. A little later,
the Japanese Apricot (*Prunus mume*) overhead, like the

Hazel oblivious to frost, makes us wonder what its delicious aroma reminds us of – no two people think alike on this. I keep sarcococcas near my front door, to get a whiff of their scent as I go and come. They are lowly evergreens with little obvious beauty of flower, whereas *Viburnum farreri* (which used to be called *V. fragrans*) smothers itself with pinky-white flowers whose fragrance travels for yards. I find that a few twigs of *Cistus × cyprius* plucked in the winter spread a warm scent of laudanum in centrally-heated rooms; the twigs last for many days.

In full spring there are the azaleas, and no species or hybrid is sweeter or stronger than the old yellow *Rhododendron luteum* (*Azalea pontica*). Tree lupins (*Lupinus arboreus*) have a sweet carrying odour, as does the tender *Cytisus racemosus*, which will thrive in warm districts. Then there are those queens of spring, *Magnolia sinensis*, *M. wilsonii* and *M. sieboldii*. A look into their snow-white cups reveals the crimson stamens, and their fragrance is fresh and lovely.

Honeysuckles are all strong candidates for inclusion – particularly *Lonicera japonica* 'Halliana', an evergreen with cream flowers from June onwards, *L. periclymenum* 'Belgica' ('Early Dutch'), 'Serotina' ('Late Dutch'), my own namesake, and *L. × americana* – but their scent is not really at its most powerful until the evening, attracting moths with a long proboscis to reach the honey in their tubes. Another wonderful scent, of richest honey, is to be savoured in later summer evenings from the long green catkins of *Itea ilicifolia*, a prickly but handsome evergreen shrub for a warm corner.

Used as a summer bedding plant or grown in pots and vases, I can think of few more delicious smells than that of Heliotrope (*Heliotropium peruvianum*), but you must have one of the well-known scented varieties like 'The

Speaker' or 'Chatsworth' – 'The Speaker' speaks to you from afar, but some of the rich-purple seed strains do not.

At the crown of the year there are of course the several white Mock Oranges or *Philadelphus*. Most are fragrant, with good carrying power, but those having purplish eyes may be particularly relied upon – such as 'Purpureo-Maculatus', 'Belle Étoile', 'Sybille', and 'Beauclerk'. With these may be grown another sun-lover, *Ozothamnus ledifolius*. This has little beauty of flower but the tiny khaki-green leaves are yellow-backed, like the stems, and exude in warm weather a rich fruity odour reminiscent of beeswax. We have already recalled the Sweet Briar and the Synstylae roses; to them we must add the old 'Albertine' and older 'Reine des Violettes', while several newer roses of David Austin's raising, particularly 'Constance Spry', have a far-carrying myrrh scent. The Rugosa roses are also worthy of note. *Lilium candidum* and *L. pyrenaicum* have strong scents that will flow across the garden; in my previous garden the latter grew near to *Philadelphus coronarius* 'Aureus', and it was difficult to separate the two penetrating aromas. One evening I was assailed by a wonderful lemony scent, from the evergreen *Magnolia* 'Maryland', a worthy hybrid of the great, cream-coloured *M. grandiflora*; its other parent, *M. virginiana*, has an equally far-carrying scent. They all need good summers to make them flower freely, which 'Maryland' will do from an early age, while *M.* × *wiesneri* (*M.* 'Watsonii') is equally strong and good in scent.

We are now approaching autumn, when *Lilium auratum* and *L. speciosum* are delicious on the air, as is the great Chinese Privet, *Ligustrum quihoui*. It has a strong claim on my affections. I know of no late August-flowering shrub with so many assets – but it is a very large grower, achieving at least 12 ft × 12 ft. Then there is the tender *Buddleja auriculata*, whose tiny cream flowers spread their scent liberally. Nor are the more usual buddlejas to be despised; if it were only for their attractiveness to butterflies, they would be worth growing.

By September one may start looking for the sweet blooms of the clerodendrons: *C. foetidum*, the suckering shrub for warm corners, sickly sweet in dark pink, and the much larger shrubs *C. fargesi* and *C. trichotomum*. The second has the more handsome leaves, though those of the former are tinted with purple; both have intriguing white flowers in red calyces and in good seasons are followed by blue berries. On sunny walls I give high praise to *Trachelospermum jasminoides*, its small jasmine-like flowers exuding the fragrance of the white Jasmine from a vigorous, shiny-leafed evergreen. *Clematis rehderiana* and *C. veitchiana* shed a whiff of cowslips in early autumn and – bringing us full circle once more – in spring *C. montana* in the pink variety 'Elizabeth' has a lovely, delicate smell.

In late July there comes a day when the summit of the season is past; there are still plenty of insects for fledglings to pursue and gobble up, but their parents mostly stop singing. It is a sad moment when neither thrush nor blackbird is heard. Even the robin, which has been singing non-stop through autumn, winter and spring, falls silent. Then is the time when, during the slumberous afternoons and evenings of late summer, the wood pigeon's song is most appreciated, and somehow appropriate. An old friend of mine used to say that they would perch in the trees at the end of his vegetable garden and sing gloatingly at him, after a feast among his rows of produce,

> *Your* peas, you fool,
> Your *green* peas, you fool,
> Your *best* peas, you fool,
> Huh?

And then, after a pause, 'poor foo-ool – poor foo-ol'. In country districts the pigeons are echoed by the clamorous cawing of rooks.

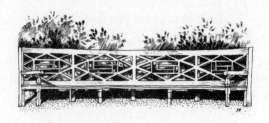

CHAPTER SIX

Ornaments for the garden

Sculpture in a garden is to be regarded not as an ornament but almost as a necessity, as like that last touch of
colour in a picture which sets the whole canvas in a
flame.

From *On the Making of Gardens*
by Sir George Sitwell (1949)

WE CAN ENJOY flowers wherever they may be,
adorning trees and shrubs, in borders and beds –
and in containers. Certainly in the awakening weeks of
the year we particularly appreciate pots and vases filled
with wallflowers, polyanthuses and bulbs, to be
removed when past their best and replaced by other
plants, for summer display. However, since its *raison
d'être* is to hold plants, a container that is empty (except,
perhaps, if it is an elaborate historical piece) strikes a
neglected note in the garden, and should be avoided.

Garden ornaments may be used for several purposes:
to bring colour to a paved area; to act as a focal point to
a designed portion of the garden; to offer the unex-

pected; or simply to give a formal emphasis to a completely informal area (the most difficult of achievements). But wherever it is placed, make sure that the right sort of ornament – vase, sundial, urn, seat, or any other worthy object – be chosen to make the emphasis most appropriately. Plant-lovers find containers of any sort filled with flowers particularly attractive, but there are times and places when something more austere may be the better choice.

Immediately we think of that favourite in gardens, the sundial. Sundials are particularly linked with gardens and borders of flowers open to the sun where its rays will catch them for as long as possible each day – they would be of little use in a shaded woodland garden – and some of the most elaborate sundials are to be found in the great gardens of Scotland, where the daylight hours in summer are longer than in the south.

We can imagine man, at the very outset of civilisation, noticing how the shadows from the sun made a special point at the waning of the day's light, and from those early beginnings no doubt stemmed the invention of our earliest time-pieces, perhaps a circle of stones with a tree branch near the centre to act as the time-teller. This was brought home to me at about the age of fourteen, when a percipient physics master first fired my imagination to make a sundial, having due regard to the North Pole and Magnetic North; I became involved with right-angles, perspective, circles, planes and all the rest, and to this day have the dial, made out of a square of lead. On it were scratched deeply the points of the compass, in Gothic initials, and the twelve hours, the quarters marked by Roman figures. My brother was called in for the making of the *gnomon*. Miraculously, it worked, and still tells the time to the nearest few minutes.

Any sort of stone, however it may be used in a garden,

is certainly the absolute antithesis of wayward plant forms, a fundamental contrast of the weak and the strong, exemplified by the trail of ivy which clings where it can to stone, or the small plant which invades any crack in paving. In a sundial it is echoed, somewhat paradoxically, in the contrast between the weathering, softening stone and the obdurate bronze of dial and *gnomon*. Here is nature's subterfuge played off against man's use of unyielding materials. As a garden ornament the sundial recalls the blessed hour, the passage of time never to be repeated, and brings thoughts which have their foundation in the immensity of time and space. It gathers all thoughts into one; perhaps this is the reason for its enduring popularity in gardens. 'The dial should stand in a space open to the heavens and its motto be worthy of the heaven of the soul that surveys it. In its presence we should feel the presence of the Eternal, and the spirit of the motto should be true to the human heart, above its sorrows and trials, reaching to daily experience and highest hopes' (from Lancelot Cross, *The Book of Old Sundials and their Mottoes*, 1922).

> Shadow and sun, so too our lives are made,
> Yet think how great the sun, how small the shade.

It is one thing to have a garden filled with flowers and interesting artefacts, but it is also necessary for it to exert its influence on the viewer. It should attract as well as be attractive. To be able to survey the whole garden on entering it does *not* attract: we need to be enticed into it to discover its full character. There is no surer way of achieving this then to arrange hedges and shrubs so that it is necessary to take a stroll to come upon its hidden areas. Some form of screen, with perhaps a gate or door in it, is also ideal in separating one part of the garden from another where, perhaps, the choice and style of planting may be totally different, or the colours a complete change. For any of these purposes, a solid door is my ultimate choice. Many would choose a wrought-iron gate, but this allows one to gain an impression of what is beyond before opening it. To me there is nothing so effective as a wooden door to give a full stop and finish to one view before what is revealed on opening the door is glimpsed. I have known several gardens thus divided, and the delight experienced by visitors is the reward.

The door needs to be well-finished and traditional in shape, preferably with a curved top rail, either convex or concave. It needs to be well hung and have a hasp that easily closes, to avoid damage in high winds. All this presupposes stout immovable posts or, preferably, brick pillars – and the next thought is that the eye and brain demand that such posts or pillars support something, such as a wall or fence, or a dense hedge of yew or holly. This all adds up to what is obviously a major feature – but one I think worth considering in all but the smallest gardens.

With statuary, as with all other sorts of garden artefacts, there are numerous copies of the real thing to be had in cast imitation stone; a genuine carved stone statue is a possession usually inherited, as original statues are enormously expensive. Many people cannot in any case tell the difference between an original and a well-weathered cast copy, so good are some reproductions. If you hanker after a life-size statue, you must first consider whether your garden deserves such an embellishment. While a sundial or vase can be an appropriate ornament for the average garden, a statue of considerable size may upset its quality and balance. It is a subject that needs careful consideration.

Garden receptacles of considerable size made of stone or other material have come to be called urns, but this used not to be so; strictly speaking, an urn is a comparatively small receptacle *with a lid*, intended to contain the ashes of the dead. Open-topped vases or bowls invite you to fill them with flowering plants to give a glorious uplift to any appropriate garden scene; but I feel that an urn, from its original nature, is more suited to a shady and retiring position, somewhere its melancholy connotations will be emphasised by evergreens, perhaps. An old round which I used to sing goes:

> Wind, gentle evergreen, to form a shade, around the
>   tomb where Sophocles is laid;
> Sweet ivy, bend thy boughs, and intertwine with
>   blushing roses and the clust'ring vine.

It is very much a poem extolling the beauty of the ivy, and finishes with the line 'Thus will thy lasting leaves, with beauties hung, prove grateful emblems of the lays he sung.' There is no doubt that the ivy with its pretty trails of small leaves clinging here and there brings just the right touch to a pedestal supporting an urn. But on no account let it engulf the shaft: this would destroy the picture, and in their removal the clinging adventitious roots will destroy the surface patina. Ordinary ivy will most likely arrive of its own accord, and brings with it a charm of leafy trail not equalled by any other plant – so long as it is strictly under control. If planting ivy, you should choose one of the smaller-leafed variants, like 'Caenwoodiana' or 'Très Coupé'.

An urn is best placed where one comes upon it as a surprise around a bend in a path or enshrouded with evergreens, both shrubs and ferns. Gardens need a contrast in mood and shape such as this to set off blossoms elsewhere, and the sudden change to darkness and greenery can be very effective, even in a small garden. In such bosky shelter many shrubs would thrive; the Alexandrian Laurel, for instance (*Danaë racemosa*), not a laurel at all but a distinguished member of the Lily family, with its elegant, arching sprays of shining ever-green leaves, sometimes bearing small red berries. Its close relative the Butchers' Broom (*Ruscus aculeatus*) will, in its hermaphrodite form, give you handsome red berries even in dense shade. Its vernacular name comes from its use when tied into dense bunches – the prickly leaves provided good scourers for wooden tables before stout brushes came to be made. Evergreen ferns assort well with ivies and shrubs, giving a nice contrast of shape and helping to create that 'sweet melancholy' we are seeking.

If there is no suitable boskage, or my suggestions seem too restrained, urns can of course be placed in full sunshine, simply as an ornament. In such a position there is no doubt that the company of Rosemary suits them best.

CHAPTER SEVEN

Flowers for early summer, and perhaps for autumn?

WE HAVE TO wait till early June in England for all risk of frost to abate, and then is the time to bring out the tender summer flowers, in the hope that soft warm rain will fall. Often just the opposite happens: June can be cold and dry. It is however a delectable period, with bird-song and the leafing of trees and a general sense of summer arriving.

It is also a busy time in the garden. Nothing stands still, and there are always jobs to be done. Not the least is weeding; my maxim is never to allow them to flower, still less to set seed, and this calls for constant vigilance. Fast-growing shoots of various clematises need securing and training, as they quickly get into a tangle. Roses, both climbers and ramblers, put out strong young growths which often need a tie or two to ensure they will grow where they are most wanted. There is no pause in the gardening round.

Summer is the time to order autumn-flowering bulbs, which should mostly be planted by the end of August, before they start sprouting. Among the first to flower are some of the crocuses, and I know few more cheering sights in September than the veined deep lilac cups of *Crocus speciosus* opening in warm sunshine to show their orange stigmata. This is quick of increase, and a number of special colour forms have been named, such as 'Aitchesonii' and the richly coloured violet-blue 'Oxonian'. With them one can have *C. kotschyanus* in pale lilac; both these species are suitable for naturalising in any sunny slope in well-drained soil. *Crocus nudiflorus* and *C. byzantinus* (*C. iridiflorus*) are two other good generous species to try. I find the latter seems to appreciate some shade. Its old name calls attention to the strangely shaped flowers whose inner three segments are much shorter than the outer ones, giving them something of the outline of an iris. Later into the autumn, these species link up with *C. laevigatus*, of which the variety *fontenayi* is usually grown. The dainty little flowers of cool lilac are striped outside and have a pronounced sweet fragrance. Half a dozen in a wine glass will scent an entire room.

The one difficulty with these little bulbs is to know how to place them so that their long leaves, appearing after the flowers, will not be too obtrusive. If they are naturalised in short grass all is well, but in borders of other treasures it is as well to grow them among such dwarf covering plants as *Cotula* or *Acaena*, which will also help to guard against rain-splashing, or with a dwarf, carpeting, silvery-leafed *Artemisia* like *A. stelleriana* or *A. pedemontana*. These silvery plants thrive in sunny spots and make the ideal foil for the colours of the crocuses.

Far more difficult to place are the so-called 'autumn crocuses', which also thrive in sunny positions but are really colchicums and are related to the lilies, not to the crocuses. It will be noticed that they have six stamens to the three of the crocuses, while the bulbs are large and covered with dark brown tunics like those of tulips, quite distinct from the netted tunics of crocus corms. Their leaves are as large as those of tulips and grow with great rapidity in spring. Few gardeners have a good word to say for these leaves, but to my eyes they are welcome as almost the first rich green thing of any size to appear in the early year – just when the daffodils start to flower and before the grass has assumed its fresh colouring. There is no doubt that the ideal way to grow these bulbs is in rough grass, where they will have a green background (for appearance and anti-splash) and where their great leaves later will do no harm – they occasionally seed themselves, but normally have to be lifted in summer and pulled apart for replanting.

The British native species *Colchicum autumnale* is one of the lesser lights of the genus, but amenable and free-flowering. Like all the other autumn-flowering species they will flower on a shelf or table, without being planted, and thus make ideal gifts for the young, or the old. All the species have large rosy-lilac flowers, often with white throats. Some of the finest are *C. byzantinum* and *C. speciosum* and the hybrid 'Atrorubens', the last a warm deep purplish rose. But the queen of the entire tribe is undoubtedly *C. speciosum* 'Album', whose great globular flowers are of gleaming creamy-white, borne on tall stout stalks. I have grown with satisfaction two doubles, the hybrid 'Water Lily' in rosy lilac and the smaller *C. autumnale* 'Flore Pleno Album'. A rare small species, *C. variegatum*, has distinctly chequered segments, like those of *Fritillaria meleagris*, which character it has passed on to its hybrids *C. agrippinum* and the handsome 'Disraeli'. Taking them all together – and there are many more – the colchicums are easy of cultivation (they seem to thrive in any reasonably drained soil), and bring a refreshing touch to the early autumn garden. They tone in well with hardy fuchsias, Japanese anemones and *Sedum spectabile*, and can thus be used to give a fine send-off to summer.

Early summer is the best time to plant nerines, those notable bulbs from South Africa. *Nerine bowdenii* is the best known and the hardiest; 'Fenwick's Variety' is perhaps the most satisfactory and free-flowering. But if you garden in a moist climate like that of the British Isles, give them a spot at the foot of a sunny wall. There the bulbs will increase and gradually push themselves above the soil, entrancing you with the most elegant, crisped lily-flowers in warm rosy pink, carried on tall stems. I have to put up with their effect against my reddish bricks, which always makes me wish the bricks were of stone colour. The modest leaves appear in spring.

So the ordering of bulbs to flower in late summer and autumn will keep us busy during the cold evenings of May and June. Meanwhile the perennial plants are waking up and beginning to compete with the flowering shrubs, which are perhaps at their best during these months.

Those two great glories of the June garden, the irises and peonies, jostle for pride of place with aquilegias, the lavender *Salvia haematodes* and flaming *Geranium psilostemon*. My own preferences in irises are not the over-frilled and goffered Tall Bearded varieties, but those kinds which still exhibit the grace and shape of the species. I particularly like those of the Spuria section, tall plants at 3 to 4 feet with elegant, strongly recurved falls – *I. orientalis*, 'Ochraurea', 'Cambridge Blue' – and also the foot-high *I. kerneriana*, an exquisite miniature. They all seem to prosper in any fertile soil, and are good 'landscape' plants, adding a vertical line and assorting well with shrubs and plants. They make specially good companions for the earlier Old Roses.

Aquilegias are best appreciated I think in the Long Spurred hybrid strains embracing almost all colours including blue, yellow, crimson and white. Not for me the 'Clematiflora' strain without spurs, the character which gives the greatest charm to these plants. If you look closely the spurred flowers resemble birds, hence *Aquilegia* (*Aquila* = eagle) and Columbine (*Columba* = dove). They are not long-lived, but sow themselves about.

Few plants give a more powerful effect in the June garden than *Salvia haematodes*, with upright spikes of coolest pale lavender, and *Geranium psilostemon*, forming great round cushions with its multitudes of flaming magenta flowers enriched by black centres; both have excellent foliage. Not even the bounties of July can surpass the garden effect of these two splendid plants, and as a foil to their display I like *Anthericum liliago*, St Bernard's Lily, a clump-former with grassy leaves and spires of small white lily-flowers, best in *A. l.* 'Major' (sometimes called *A. algeriense*).

As to peonies, they are imposing plants in foliage and flower, thriving in any good soil in full sun; in fact, some of the best plants I have ever seen were in a grassy meadow-garden. Like all these early summer flowerers they are best planted in early autumn, so that they can get their roots well down before coping with the demands their lavish display of blossom makes on them. One of the earliest to flower is *P. obovata alba*. Wild species such as this, being singles, have a short life in flower but couple that with a charm and opulence which can astonish us, so lately nourished on Narcissi and tulips. *Paeonia obovata alba* has pure white chalices centred on a bunch of yellow stamens around bulky, downy carpels capped with crimson. The diaphanous white of the flowers has its counterpart in the soft dove-tint of the leaves, which surprise us by continuing to grow in their rounded shape even after the flowers have dropped.

Nobody who has attempted to pronounce the name of *P. mlokosewitschii* will be likely to forget this superlative single, light canary-yellow species. It has no rival in the gardening world. Paler but of almost equal charm is the larger *P. wittmanniana*. This has given rise in the hands of the French nurseryman Lemoine to several exquisite hybrids, headed by the lovely 'Avant Garde', whose soft opalescent pink flowers tone so well with the coppery foliage; it is a tall stout grower. *Paeonia arietina* heads a group of magenta-pink species, of which *P. daurica* is a prominent member. Both have soft greyish green leaves which assort well with the flower-colour, but *P. arietina* has a tendency to vary to soft pale rose, one of which such forms has been named, appropriately, 'Mother of Pearl'.

I give high marks to *P. emodi*, whose gracious white blooms and pale green leaves light the early May garden, quickly followed by a shorter plant, from China, *P. veitchii*, in magenta-pink, and its paler rose-pink variant *woodwardii*. This has elegantly cut leaves, but not so finely cut as those of *P. tenuifolia* from the Caucasus. This has flowers of crimson; perhaps better known is its double form, and there is also a pink form, of great rarity. Their very finely cut leaves are somewhat inherited by the noteworthy hybrids × *smouthii* and 'Early Bird', two vivid crimson singles with silky segments. Much brighter in tone is *P. peregrina*, of which there are two forms in general cultivation, a particularly vivid red in 'Fire King' (*P. lobata*), and a keen sort of coral-scarlet in 'Sunshine'. Apart from certain tulips, no flowers at that time of the year can compete with them for brilliance, and they lead us on to the old double crimson peony of cottage gardens (and my own!), *P. officinalis* 'Rubra Plena' and its relatives. I have a special weakness for 'Anemoneflora Rosea', whose red-cupped petals hold in their centre petaloid stamens, to which we shall recur later. There is a vivid hybrid with *P. peregrina*, called 'China Rose', which has bold flowers of coral-pink.

One of the glories of the early peony season is that ancient Chinese cultivar *P. lactiflora* (*P. albiflora*) 'The Bride', which ushers in the garden races with great charm and vigour. To my mind there are few peonies to compare with the beauty of its traditional noble dark foliage and wide milk-white flowers, almost single, with handsome centres of yellow stamens. For long Messrs Lemoine in France and Messrs Kelway of Langport in Somerset were the leaders in hybridising those magnificent plants, the heavyweight doubles of the garden races, evolved from *P. lactiflora* and old varieties bred ages ago in China and Japan. It is not surprising that these plants have always been popular, for when well cultivated they have a compelling and unique attraction. The darkest colour – like blackcurrant juice – is one known as 'Hidcote Purple'; rather nearer to mulberry is 'Monsieur Martin Cahusac'. There are splendid crimsons and pinks, blushes and whites – 'Duchesse de Nemours' is pure white, while 'Festiva Maxima' is decorated with an occasional crimson fleck in the centre.

Of all the older peonies – mostly raised a hundred years or more ago – few equal the charm of the race bred by Kelways and which they called Imperial Peonies. I mentioned in connection with *P. officinalis* a variety with petaloid stamens, and it is this striking characteristic that the Imperials have inherited. These stamens, in part narrow petals, give the flowers an indescribable richness of yellow and other tints, without qualifying them as being really double.

The tide of hybridising passed during the twentieth century from Europe to the United States. Species were reassessed and numerous crosses, likely and unlikely, were made by Dr A.P. Saunders of New York and his daughter. I have already mentioned 'Early Bird', which is typical of the delectable singles that were raised; others such as 'Rose Garland' and 'Defender' are already known in European gardens. A great boost has also been given to garden hybrids by the firm of Messrs Klehm of Illinois. Their catalogue is a revelation of what may be done in this august genus, and includes what they call their Estate Peonies – great, strong, upstanding hybrids of every possible shape, colour and size – and also another race partly evolved by another breeder, one William Krekner, of dwarf hybrids, covering a wide range of colours and form, suitable for smaller gardens as they seldom exceed 2 feet in height.

While writing these notes I have had constantly in the back of my mind what admirable garden and landscape plants these all are. There is a thrill in seeing their knobbly, often reddish buds in spring, unfurling into beautiful leaves which create a firm background for the great flowers. Once the dead flower heads have been removed, they still add nobly to our borders with their bold, fingered leaves which last in beauty until early autumn. They are therefore, I think, to be classed among the best of plants for their landscape value throughout the season.

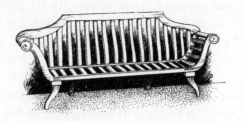

CHAPTER EIGHT

The later rhododendrons

IN THE SOUTH of England, June brings us the most floriferous and showy of rhododendrons, the so-called Hardy Hybrids, which will grow from 6 to 12 feet tall and as much in width. Apart from the precocious 'Pink Pearl' and 'Cynthia' – two of the most popular of all kinds – they flower with us when spring is going past and summer approaches. But space is needed to accommodate their dark evergreen bushes laden with flowers. The most admirable use of these rather overpowering shrubs that I have seen is at Lochinch in south-west Scotland, where they fit perfectly into the rolling landscape, with lots of greenery around them. It is so different a planting that one can forget these are the same large shrubs responsible for the stodgy lumps of colour to be seen in some of our small southern gardens. There is no doubt that wherever they are planted and allowed to reach full maturity they dominate the scene when in flower; their foliage, however, is rather stark and gloomy.

But there is no clear-cut division into earlies and lates, and many of the groups, not excepting the famous

Waterer Hardy Hybrids, overlap both ways. Thus some of them will be in flower in late spring with the flaming azaleas, while others will not bloom for several weeks. And this of course is where danger lies, in garden and landscape planting – the old, ever-present problem of avoiding clashes of colour between those whose flowers lean towards the yellow end of the spectrum and those with a colour bias towards the blue, which is found in all the hardy hybrids of the Waterer breed. Past and fallen are those valuable blenders 'Loder's White', *R. yunnanense*, the lavender-blue 'Susan' and my own namesake, raised by his father and named for me by Donald Waterer; gone too are the exquisite 'Penjerrick', in soft yellow or pink, and all the refined *R. soulei* hybrids. Some delicacy is to be found in certain hybrids of *R. yakushimanum*, though unsuitable mating with large-flowered hybrids has produced a very mixed bag, among which there are many devoid of the joyous refinement of this species from southern Japan. I hope its sister species, the elegant *R. pseudochrysanthum*, may fare better. It is another paragon of beauty in flower and foliage which will take a lot of beating.

So the stage is set for the old Hardy Hybrids, what the average gardener calls to mind when rhododendrons are mentioned. They carry with them an inherent disadvantage – most are propagated by grafting onto rootstocks of the mauve *R. ponticum*, and unless this grafting is expertly done, so that no suckers accrue, in a mixed assembly there will nearly always be some suckers appearing. Among rhododendrons the mauve will not clash, but unfortunately – as azaleas and rhododendrons are almost always planted together, and to excess, wherever they thrive – azaleas are often produced by grafting too. In this case it is *R. luteum* (*Azalea pontica*) that is used. This wonderful free-flowering, richly scented plant, also noted for its splendid autumn colour, opens its strong warm-yellow flowers at the same time as those early Hybrid rhododendrons, such as the already mentioned 'Pink Pearl' and 'Cynthia', with either of which it makes a strident contrast. Some nurserymen, however, produce their named azaleas and rhododendrons from layers; the resulting young plants are not always quite so shapely, but this is a small disadvantage, soon outgrown, compared with the liability to sucker.

The best of these Hardy Hybrid rhododendrons are household names: blazing 'Britannia', the huge pink 'Betty Wormald' and 'Marinus Koster', palest 'Gomer Waterer' and 'Sweet Simplicity'; rich dark violet 'Royal Purple', which has more life in its tint than the better-known 'Purple Splendour'; and darkest 'Frank Galsworthy', a fruity red-purple with a unique yellowish green flare in the throat – a suitable variety to commemorate a water-colour artist of great skill.

Though the general scene is dominated by the Waterer Hybrids, this does not mean that the later-flowering species can be forgotten. It is these and their immediate hybrids that are mainly fancied by rhododendron buffs today; there is a charm and refinement about them not found in the Hardy Hybrids. These suit the suburban scene well enough and put up with considerable sun, but the later species on the whole are better suited to the woodland they prefer, where the sun's increasing power is mitigated by overhead shade, and their less overweening display suits such woodland flowers as Solomon's Seal and white foxgloves, and the delicacy of ferns. I should not like to have a large garden without the glories of such as white and blush *R. decorum* and *R. discolor*, 'Mrs A.T. de la Mare' and the Loder 'King George', 'Pink Diamond' and others of that voluptuous breed. They all have rich scent and echo the gracious beauty of trumpet lilies. But they are now going over, to be followed in June by the no less beautiful 'Angelo' hybrids, so much in evidence at Sheffield Park in Sussex. All of these are white or palest pink and lighten the woodland glades, a direct contrast to certain red species and hybrids. These are much valued for their stunning reflection in the lake at Mount Stewart, Northern Ireland. It would startle the most phlegmatic mortal to see the colour of *R. thomsonii* reflected amongst the tender spring greenery, a flaming torch of glowing rich crimson. The flowers have been likened to burning coals. They belong to the earlier weeks, but fortunately the vivid effect can be repeated by using several later species, such as the renowned pair *R. elliottii* and *R. facetum* (which used to be called *R. eriogynum*). They both make large bushes up to some 12 feet and are spectacular with their somewhat tubular flowers of brilliant red. Much smaller, but equally telling in the garden landscape, are *R. neriiflorum* and *R. beanianum*, both red.

Now we should I think consider some modern hybrids. There are several of fierce red tint, some approaching orange and shrimp pink, inherited from *R. griersonianum* and *R. dichroanthum*. The former species has revolutionised the colouring of hybrids, imparting a warm almost coppery tone to its progeny, whereas from the latter some strange orange tones have emanated, coupled with the Canterbury Bell form of flower – a trumpet with a cup round it. Most of the latter are lowly bushes, while *R. griersonianum* is the parent of both large and small growers, witness 'Aladdin' and 'Vanessa'. They all bring us the sharp colours normally found rather among azaleas than in the general run of rhododendrons. By late June in Surrey comes the rich dark red of 'Grosclaude' with its sumptuous bell-flowers; a low bush, it gives a wonderful contrast to the cream flowers of *Magnolia* × *thompsoniana*. This magnolia is well worthy of more frequent choice in gardens: not only does it flower well after spring frosts are past, but it has inherited from one of its parents – *M. virginiana* – a most glorious fragrance.

As the rhododendron season draws to its close I very much bless certain azaleas. Not only do they flower late and extend the season, but their colourings blend well with the rather bright rhododendrons mentioned, and most are well scented. *Rhododendron occidentale* itself has lovely dark glossy leaves and freely-borne creamy flowers touched with pink in the bud, and is notably scented, with a long flowering season. Following closely on is *R. viscosum*, of which I specially like the form 'Glaucum', whose white, scented flowers blend so well with its glaucous grey leaves. They form a delightful picture if grouped with *Hosta sieboldiana*. Also late-flowering are such species as *R. oblongifolium* and *R. alabamense*, scented, comparatively small-growing and of warm coppery pink tint, followed by *R. prunifolium*, of rich brick-red tint, which carries on well into July. In its tint this brings to mind the Indicum azaleas, ever-green and low growing. In spite of being closely related to the florists' azaleas sold at Christmas, they are hardy in Surrey. A noted salmon-pink is 'Bungonishiki', while 'Crispiflorum' is a brilliant 'shocking' pink. Much more dwarf is the little *R. nakaharae*, whose dark foliage gives just the right background to the rich brick-red of the flowers; it is only a few inches high, but of much greater width.

But it is back to traditional rhododendrons for our last paragraph. Of tree-like habit is the magnificent scented white 'Polar Bear', often in flower in August or later. It has fine lily-like flowers inherited from its renowned parent *R. auriculatum*, again white and richly scented but of wide, thrusting, tabular growth and splendid foliage, which makes no effort to appear afresh until the flowers are over. They are both giants in their way and bring fittingly to a close this rather cursory look into the wide ramifications of a genus which – given a friable acid soil – provides us gardeners with plants for a wide variety of uses in furnishing the landscape of the garden. And when the flowers are over we still have beauty of leaf in shape and colour, except from the Hardy Hybrids, which are apt to be overwhelmingly dark and gloomy.

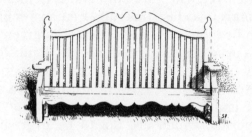

CHAPTER NINE

Large leaves for creating perspective

I SUPPOSE IT is a form of greed – and greed is at the bottom of most of mankind's endeavours – which makes us all not only long for a large garden, but also wish our garden were larger than it is; however, we need not despair. Much can be done by suggestion, and an illusion of space can be created by the use of suitable foliage. Trees of an avenue, like the pillars of a cathedral, lead the eye along and accentuate the distance, and the careful use of foliage can have the same effect: the minute leaves of a mossy tump or a densely clipped yew hedge seem infinitely farther away than the broad blades of a giant rhododendron or magnolia. I propose to explore this phenomenon, and see just how perspective can be enhanced by the thoughtful use of leaves, mainly during summer and early autumn.

Leaves, after all, are some of the most permanent things in a garden landscape, for twelve months if evergreen and perhaps six if deciduous. They are with us, in either case, for much longer than the flowers, and we cannot garden without them, so they need our closest attention in the consideration of suitable planting for any given spot. In a cursory glance over a garden prospect, large leaves catch and hold the eye while tiny leaves recede into the background. And so, to foster our idea of a larger garden, it is as well to keep plants with the biggest leaves in the foreground, leaving the tiny leaves of, say, heathers and most conifers in the background. Thereby we shall deceive the eye into thinking the garden larger than it is, without in any way creating more work.

To take my usual procedure of treating with the largest plants first, we may as well begin with a few large-leafed trees, of which likewise the first will be the largest growers; because of their natural size, the garden in which they are set needs to be of reasonable extent. It is an interesting point that really large trees, such as chestnuts or planes, do not *appear* to have exceptional leaves, as they are in scale with the size of the tree. Foliage-size becomes more dominant when considering trees of medium growth, such as the catalpas, paulownias and *Magnolia macrophylla*. I knew one keen lover of big leaves who annually cut his *Paulownia* and his *Ailanthus* down to ground level to achieve stout 8–foot-high growths parading immense leaves, but of course no flowers. This practice strays into what used to be called 'subtropical gardening', in which such grand growths vied for importance with those of palms and cannas in public parks.

Paulownia fargesii, a Chinese tree, is generally looked upon as the most satisfactory of the species for our climate in the British Isles (Zone 7 in the United States). It has thick stout branches and is a rapid grower, reaching a considerable girth in a few years. Its flower buds, formed at the ends of the branches in the autumn, by early spring enlarge into pyramidal spikes of lavender-blue foxglove-like flowers, exhaling a sweet scent even when they have fallen on the ground. The leaves, which open later, are large and palmate. There is no doubt that it is a very handsome tree, thriving in any fertile soil.

The same may be said of the catalpas, with equally large leaves and thick stems; they are not quite so vigorous, and thrive best in sunny open positions on well-drained soils. The best known is *Catalpa bignonioides*, of considerable height and wide-spreading growth, a wonderful sight when in full flower in late summer, again with terminal spikes of elegant, white, mouthed flowers, prettily marked inside with purple and orange, but giving a general effect of pale lilac. Similar is *C. speciosa*, less conspicuously marked and of rather narrow upright growth. A form of *C. bignonioides* with foliage of bright yellow in early summer – they all come into leaf late – is named *C. b.* 'Aurea'; unless well covered with flowers, following a preceding hot summer, it is apt to look a bit insipid. A hybrid, *C.* × *erubescens*, has foliage of dark coppery purple when young. The most beautiful in flower is the rosy pink *C. fargesii*, but its leaves are smaller and it lacks vigour; *C. ovata* is paler in flower, and some weeks later.

Some other trees of medium size with similar large broad leaves are *Idesia polycarpa*, *Populus lasiocarpa* and *Sorbus thibetica* 'John Mitchell'. The main attraction of the first, apart from its leaves, lies in the skeins of red berries borne on female trees in autumn. The *Sorbus*, named after the famous curator of Westonbirt Arboretum in Gloucestershire, is in the Aria or Whitebeam section of the genus, and has exceptionally large round leaves of grey-green. As to the poplar, it is a magnificent tree which bears its large leaves on red stalks.

The Tulip Tree (*Liriodendron tulipifera*) is well known but makes too large a tree for the average garden. Instead of ending in a point, the large, lobed leaves are cut off; if a growing shoot (enclosed in pale green bracts) is opened, it will be seen that this abrupt end is to give space for the next leaf when all are folded in the bud.

Apart from these several broad-leafed trees there are also trees with extra large pinnate leaves. *Ailanthus glandulosa* can be cut down annually, like the *Paulownia*, but as it is a naturally suckering tree, the result might be more stems than you desire! It is important to get a female tree, which not only has bunches of bright reddish pods in early autumn but happily lacks the rather evil smell of the male flowers. It is a tree of imposing proportions. A Walnut of fine carriage and large leaves is *Juglans cinerea*, from eastern North America. Doubly pinnate leaves of great size are found in the Kentucky Coffee Tree, *Gymnocladus dioica*, in *Meliosma veitchiorum* and *Aralia elata* and *A. chinensis*. Scarcely trees, these yet have tree-like growth, and are elegant in cream flower in summer and attractive in autumn colour with their conspicuous racemes of nearly black berries. The queen of all these doubly pinnate growths is the shining evergreen *Gevuina avellana* from Chile, but this is a tender shrub.

With large shrubs we have come to the point where we can consider *Magnolia macrophylla*, mentioned earlier. It has magnificent paddle-sized leaves and cream flowers in proportion, in summer, with a good scent. Other magnolias not quite so large are *M. tripetala* and *M. hypoleuca*: both make large shrubs, but only just could they be called trees. Their flowers are deliciously scented.

Before we turn to shrubs proper we must make a note of the two hardy palms, *Trachycarpus fortunei* and *Chamaerops humilis*. The former will make a stem of 20 feet or more in southern Britain and is conspicuous when bearing its bunches of cream flowers; the latter is seldom seen except as a shrub. Both have handsome leaves cut into fine divisions.

If we define a tree as a single-stemmed plant and a shrub as having two or more, some of the above (except for the taller Palm) should be in the latter category; but in our gardens such terminology does not really matter – what concerns us is the bulk of each plant. So let us now consider some large-growing shrubs, which take up much more space on the ground than trees, though the roots of these may spread farther. We can hardly do better than to begin with some of the greater rhododendrons, of which *R. sino-grande* takes first prize for majestic leaves, sometimes approaching 3 feet long in sheltered woodland conditions and a very mild climate. Its close relatives *R. macabeanum*, *R. falconeri* and *R. rex fictolacteum*, and others, are not so particular and grow well in most of the more sheltered conditions where rhododendrons thrive. In addition to their magnificent foliage they have large trusses of waxy, bell-shaped flowers of creamy tint, in spring.

Other evergreens for our purpose are the sun-loving magnolias, *M. delavayi* and *M. grandiflora*. While *M. delavayi* has very fine large foliage, its cream flowers are rather small in comparison; it is a Chinese species. Native to the eastern United States, *M. grandiflora*, on the other hand, has magnificent foliage *and* flowers – the leaves are hard and of shining green and rattle in the breeze, while the cream flowers are of great size and quality, and richly scented of lemon. There are several good selections, such as 'Exmouth Variety' and the noble 'Goliath'. These are propagated from cuttings and may be expected to flower in a few years, whereas seed-raised plants may take as many as twenty. Some hybrids have been raised between *M. grandiflora* and *M. virginiana*, a pleasing small shrub also with a pronounced lemony fragrance; the two I have come across are 'Maryland' and 'Freeman', and both flower when only about 3 feet high. The flowers are slightly smaller than those of 'Goliath', but of the same delicious fragrance and quality. While 'Freeman' is a comparatively upright shrub and so suitable for smaller gardens, in my experience the flowers do not open so well, nor is it so free. All of these kinds flower best in a hot summer, and are in bloom for weeks. One single flower put in a vase will scent a room of an evening.

Another remarkable evergreen is *Fatsia japonica*, which thrives as well in shade as in sun, even at the seaside. It belongs to the ivy family, and in late autumn bears most imposing ivory-white drumstick heads at the tops of the stems. Unfortunately they are often spoiled by frost. The foliage, however, is magnificent, great rounded blades divided into broad fingers. In the spring in frost-free maritime districts large clusters of nearly black fruits mature, the size of large currants. The well-known *Mahonia japonica* also takes a high place among foliage shrubs. To get the best out of it, it should be planted in the shade, though flower-arrangers might prefer to grow it in sun, for the sake of the tints which the dark green boldly pinnate (and prickly) leaves achieve. Some light is necessary to encourage the strings of lime-yellow bell-like flowers which appear from late autumn onwards, deliciously scented. In the warmer days of April their fragrance is carried far on the air.

For a sheltered corner in very mild districts there is nothing so unbelievably handsome as *Melianthus major*. In this deciduous shrubby plant the leaves are of glaucous blue-green, deeply pinnate and distinctly serrate. In most parts of Britain it would not be hardy, but in maritime districts and elsewhere in the west and in Ireland and the south-west of Scotland I can think of no plant so elegant and tropical-looking, and when in summer the great growths are crowned with spires of red-brown seeds, the picture is complete; unfortunately, the foliage has a strong fetid smell when bruised. Another plant with bold pinnate leaves of rather glaucous green is *Decaisnea fargesii*, the two parts of its name recording the memory of two famous French missionaries in China. It is a big, lax, stalky shrub, quite hardy, with sprays of greenish-yellow starry flowers followed by cobalt-blue pods the size of broad beans.

Freely seen throughout the country is *Rhus typhina*, the Staghorn Sumach, a small tree or large shrub with very splendid long, pinnate leaves borne on thick furry brown stems and turning to a resplendent scarlet in autumn, at which time the red-brown velvety seed heads on female plants are held aloft, like so many antlers, remaining in place through the winter. I suppose the most desirable form is that known as 'Dissecta', a female; the leaves are not only pinnate but also deeply cut. It is often known, erroneously, as 'Laciniata', but this name is really only applicable to a similar form of a related species, *R. glabra*. Both species spread by means of suckers. The stems of *R. glabra*, as its name suggests, entirely lack the furriness characteristic of *R. typhina*, and the velvety 'horns' are not so long-lasting as *typhina*'s, but the 'Laciniata' form is a plant of great beauty and excellence. Both species are native to North America.

Two more pinnate-leafed shrubs of large size are *Sambucus canadensis* 'Maxima', an Elder of rare beauty with great lacy heads of tiny creamy flowers followed by tiny murrey-coloured berries, and the sorbarias. These relatives of the spiraeas excel in beautiful long pinnate foliage, crowned on the summer's growths by big feathery heads of tiny cream flowers. They provide no autumn colour, nor fruits of any particular beauty, and spread by means of suckers. The most magnificent for large spaces are *Sorbaria arborea* and *S. tomentosa* (*S. lindleyana*); *S. assurgens*, *S. aitchisonii* and *S. sorbifolia* are smaller species, but with much of the same beauty.

I also think very highly of two other shrubs which, like the sorbarias above, spread by means of the rootstock; both have fine large hand-like leaves on stems not unlike those of a Raspberry, to which they are related. One, with white flowers, is *Rubus parviflora* (*R. nutkana*); the other, *R. odorata*, has crushed raspberry-pink (mixed with cream, of course) flowers, borne over a long period. My experience is that they thrive best in sandy or gravelly soils. A good pink hybrid of great vigour has been raised by crossing with *R.* 'Benenden', the result a larger shrub with even larger leaves and a long flowering period. A plant of considerable charm, though seldom seen, is *R. irenaeus*, which can lie flat on the ground or be trained up a support. It is ever-green, with large rounded deckle-edged leaves of rich green, pale buff-felted beneath, as are the stems. The flowers are not conspicuous but the fruiting sprays are highly ornamental, with shining red fruits and tinted calyces.

We are left with the viburnums, and *Rhamnus imeretina*. This last is not an especially showy shrub, having no beauty of flower, fruit or autumn colour, but the leaves are large and handsome; it thrives best, I think, in cool places. Of the viburnums, *V. rhytidophyllum* tops the scales for size of growth and leaf. The leaves are not only large but deeply veined, and covered with creamy brown felting beneath, to match the stems. When grown in woodland or otherwise sheltered from wind few shrubs are more eye-catching in their heads of creamy flowers and scarlet berries turning to black (there is a pink-flowered form which has not such good foliage); but in windy sites the leaves of all forms of this species become tattered and droopy. Not so *V. davidii*. Of all the shrubs under discussion this is the most admirable foreground evergreen, making domes of dark green deeply veined leaves, slowly achieving some 2 feet in height but much wider. Female forms bear heads of blue berries on reddish stalks in autumn, succeeding the white flower heads. A much taller shrub of the same attractions is *V. cinnamomifolium*, with blue-black berries.

We can include certain climbers for our purposes, which can be trained up trees, to hang down in a curtain of growth, or on arches or house walls. A warm sunny house wall could hardly be decorated with anything more bold in leaf than a Fig tree. In Britain it is only likely to fruit in the warmest districts, but even so its deeply lobed leaves are very striking. In cities and sheltered places the best fruiting sorts will make an imposing bushy tree; they do not develop any autumn colour, but their pale grey bark is very noticeable in winter.

The so-called Kiwi fruit comes not from the Antipodes but from the Chinese climber *Actinidia chinensis*. It is an immense grower and only suitable for a very high wall, or climbing into a large tree. The most handsome large-leafed climbers are various vines; *Vitis coignetiae* and *V. armata* are two Chinese species of note (there are many more, including fruiting grapes) with specially large rounded foliage. Each third leaf along a branch has a tendril for attachment to its host tree or woodwork. They do not bear serviceable fruit, but have most splendid autumn colour. Closely related is *Ampelopsis megalophylla*, with large bipinnate foliage; it also is good in autumn.

When it comes to herbaceous perennials, the ultimate in size is before us: no other plant that can be grown in Temperate Zone gardens equals *Gunnera manicata* and the slightly smaller *G. scabra*, both natives of South America. They need the widest landscape to accommodate their immense leaves – as much as 6 feet or more across, borne aloft on stout stalks. One has to go to a great landscape garden such as Sheffield Park in Sussex to realise the majesty of such leaves in the foreground, in contrast to the tranquil lake and the minute foliage of conifers in the distance – the ultimate indeed in our essay in perspective. But the gunneras are only suitable in great boggy gardens; most of us would have to make do with *Peltiphyllum* and *Rodgersia*. *Peltiphyllum peltatum* has very large orbicular leaves borne on stout stalks to 2 or 3 feet, of rich green often turning to red in autumn; they follow the elegant saxifrage-like starry heads of pink flowers which are carried on hairy stalks in early spring. The great fleshy rhizomes cover marshy ground like those of irises.

Similar orbicular leaves – again with the stalks fitted to the centre of the leaf – are found in *Astilboides tabularis*, which used to be called *Rodgersia tabularis*. Other species of *Rodgersia* have deeply divided leaves reminding one of those of the Horse Chestnut; in fact, one is called *R. aesculifolia*. In addition to their very dignified leaves they all bear, well aloft, gracious spiraea-like plumes of small creamy flowers; in the best of the lot, *R. pinnata* 'Superba', they are of rich rosy pink. The foliage of all can be a deep bronzy shade in spring and often provides autumn colour. They will only give of their best in rich soil that never gets dry.

In our process of descending the size scale of the various plants with splendid large foliage I should have mentioned earlier the ornamental rhubarbs – the species of *Rheum* – which, when grown in moist, well nurtured soil, cannot be beaten by anything less than a *Gunnera*; but their leaves are only good until about midsummer, after which they become limp and lose their beauty. There are few more exciting moments in spring than when the scarlet knobs of *R. palmatum*

'Atrosanguineum' burst through the soil and proceed to develop into broad, jagged leaves, green above and crimson below, until 6–foot stems burst into branching heads of tiny rosy-red blooms which later turn into colourful erect seed-heads. This species is variable, and some plants bear white flowers; there is also the very handsome 'medicinal' Rhubarb, *R. officinale*, with spectacular spikes of white flowers but plain green leaves not so elegantly jagged.

For boggy ditches and the fringes of rivers and ponds there are the two species of *Lysichitum*, *L. camtschatcense* and *L. americanum*, from either side of the Pacific Ocean. These are very similar in the leaves, but the former has the best, pure white flowers, like stemless large white Arum Lilies, and sweetly scented, whereas the other is yellow with a heavy, objectionable smell. The leaves of both are vast, shaped like canoe paddles, at first handsome and erect but later, into summer, flaccid and drooping. They make a striking contrast to the flat rounded leaves of water lilies. Also related to the arums are *Sauromatum guttatum* and *Symplocarpus*. The former is the intriguing 'Monarch of the East', which will produce its brownish-green arum-flowers from a dry bulb in a room. Later the fine, fingered leaves develop, of considerable size; likewise *Symplocarpus foetidus*, which enjoys a damp spot. In early spring the strange dark reddish-brown hooded flowers squat on the ground, followed by waving masses of deeply divided foot-high leaves of rich green. I have seen and grown *Podophyllum peltatum* and other species in moist ground, not far from water. The stems are bare for a foot or so, having a couple of large divided leaves under which the crystalline white or pink flowers nod, the precursors of large fleshy pink fruits: something quite out of the usual.

The Arum Lily of the greenhouse used to be called

Richardia – it is not a lily at all – and now, to make things more difficult, it should be labelled *Zantedeschia*: *Z. aethiopica* is the Lily of the Nile and is normally grown in water or in a bog, where it will luxuriate to perfection. Of late years there has become known a special form, 'Crowborough', found in a garden in the town of that name in Sussex growing in a mass along a sunny wall in rich soil. It has proved a hardy, hearty grower, and is possibly an upland form of the species. As a young plant, propagated from the bulbils which stud the tuberous roots, it will not stand frost, but appears to be hardy once the root-fangs have become deeply engaged in the soil. Everyone knows the splendid white trumpet flowers, a wonderful contrast to the deep shining green of the huge spear-shaped leaves which rise to about 5 feet, topped by the flowers. Nor is this the only form which will grow well out of water. There is 'Little Gem', only half the height; 'White Sail'; and the remarkable 'Green Goddess', whose flowers are mostly green, and very handsome, but do not make much effect in the garden. The flowers of all are lit by the yellow central spadix, and are good for cutting.

In this recital of moisture-loving plants it is interesting to come across one that grows equally well in dry or moist soil: *Trachystemon orientale*, a member of the Borage family. Like most of its relatives it has beautiful blue starry flowers, in early spring, before the leaves, which are very much like those of some of the hostas, but harshly hairy. It is a useful ground-cover of spreading habit.

One of the most elegant of all summer's plants is *Macleaya microcarpa*, known for many years as *Bocconia cordata*, a stately perennial with a running root that throws up stems over 6 feet in height, bearing most beautiful fingered leaves of glaucous green, buff beneath. Above them wave tall spires of tiny buff-coloured flowers. Its membership of the Poppy family is not at once apparent, but indicated by the reddish juice found in the roots. A species with a more compact root-stock is *M. cordata*, with flowers larger and whiter, and for those who like warm colour there is 'Coral Plume', a variant of *M. microcarpa*. Another imposing plant is *Aralia cachemerica*, with broadly doubly pinnate leaves and branching spires of tiny green flowers borne in round heads like those of Ivy. It makes a graceful clump to about 5 feet.

In shady places the broad, pleated foliage of the *Veratrum* species remains in beauty until late summer; *V. nigrum* has tall spires of chocolate-purple stars, paler in *V. viride* (green) and *V. californicum* (white). Few would refuse the *Acanthus* species a place in our gallery of plants with large elegant foliage. They are unfortunately rather invasive, but there is no denying the beauty of the deeply cut, dark green leaves. They will grow satisfactorily in shade but flower best in full sun and are, I think, at their most elegant in *A. spinosus*, which also is more free-flowering than the perhaps better-known *A. mollis*. Their flowers, borne well aloft on prickly spikes, are not unlike those of a Foxglove.

For foreground planting in stony or sandy limy soil you could not do better than the Seakale of our shores, *Crambe maritima*. Apart from its wide heads of little creamy flowers in spring it gives us the most handsome of all glaucous foliage, curved, lobed and convoluted. For part shade there are the spring-flowering Forget-me-not flowers in clear blue of *Brunnera macrophylla*. This has large rounded hairy leaves sometimes spotted with what looks like aluminium paint, especially in the form known as 'Langtrees'. These brunneras are both lowly plants. The Japanese Anemones are often recommended for shade, but I think they thrive and flower best in the open in sun, or in shade from a wall. None of the doubles or semi-doubles has the charm of the original two, *Anemone* × *hybrida* (pink) and 'Honorine Jobert' (pure white). One would need to search hard for greater floral perfection, or for more long-lasting beauty from the large divided leaves.

Some plants that love plenty of moisture are the several species of *Ligularia*, formerly *Senecio*. The best known is *L. dentata*, with great rounded leaves on tall stalks surrounding spires of orange daisy flowers up to some 4 feet. A specially richly-coloured form is known variously as 'Desdemona' or 'Othello', with the leaves tinted coppery-purple above and wholly dark beneath. Other fine species and hybrids are *L. veitchiana*, *L. stenocephala*, 'Gregynog Gold' and *L.* × *palmatiloba*; *L. hodgsonii* is for smaller gardens. The daisy breed does not stop here, for we must include *Buphthalmum speciosum*, with magnificent foliage and branching stems carrying wide, neatly-rayed orange flowers in the summer months. It has a wandering rootstock.

Cannas, formerly considered to belong to park bedding, are becoming increasingly used in our gardens for the sake of their smooth convoluted leaves enclasping erect flower stems; but for me they are something of a disappointment, being rather stiff and shapeless, for all the satisfaction that the rich colourschemes of flower and leaf give us. These strictures do not apply to *C. iridiflora*, to which the name *ehemannii* is often added. This is rather different, a grand plant, with the same attraction of suave, smooth, blue-green leaves of great size but bearing its flowers gracefully on a 5–foot stem, prettily nodding. It is not generally hardy in Britain, but easy to over-winter in pots in a frost-free building. All cannas are greedy plants – as greedy for nourishment as for water.

And so we come to those old favourites, the lowly hostas and bergenias. The latter are the plants *par excellence* for associating with paths, steps and any masonry, their large evergreen leathery leaves providing just that note of luxuriance required as a foil for building materials. In addition I also use them as a contrast to the mossy, fine-grained effect of winter-flowering heaths, dwarf cotoneasters, and hebes. The be-all and end-all of foreground planting, they provide the right introduction to perspective schemes, from the very garden door. Flowers in heads of light pink appear soon after Christmas among the large, stalked blades of *Bergenia × schmidtii* 'Ernst Schmidt', after which other kinds appear, usually darker, richer and taller. There are several good species and many hybrids, some of the best being 'Ballawley', with extra-large leaves turning to liver-colour in winter, and the richly toned *B. ligulata* with crimson-backed leaves. They are essentially sun-loving plants which will also grow well in shade, but their leaf colours will be intensified and their flowers more prolific in sun.

Now for those typical lovers of cool shady places, the hostas. Following a great surge in popularity during the last few decades, these are to be found in most gardens where the conditions are cool and the soil reasonably moist. It is difficult to see the justification for their popular name of 'plantain lilies', though lilies they are, botanically. The flowers of all kinds certainly resemble lilies in some shape or form, borne on tall stems well above the mounds of foliage, mostly in purple, pale lavender or white. And what satisfying mounds of foliage they are, too: gracious, luxuriantly arching broad leaves in positively every tone of green from rich Hooker's green to almost blue. And the variegation! Assiduous eyes have watched for and propagated every last flash or stripe or edging of white, cream or yellow, until the modern craze for ornamental foliage might well be assuaged by the variation found among hostas alone. As a complete contrast to the delicacy of green ferns they are supreme, and fill a woodland glade to perfection. Like cannas, ligularias, veratrums and a few other good plants they delight slugs and snails, so that where these abound it is well to make early applications of slug pellets, before the scrolled leaves unfurl. This is often not until early June, so that these plants are essentially for summer effect.

All these notes have been concerned with leaves used to enhance perspective and a sense of spaciousness, and leaves, as I have said, should fill our minds when planning a garden; they are the first essential and the foundation on which the garden is built. Leaves strap- or sword-shaped, leaves of lacy and filigree effect, indeed leaves of all shapes and colours, will be found in my book *The Art of Planting*.

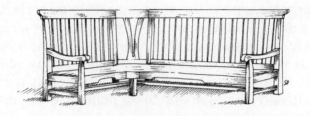

CHAPTER TEN

White roses – a review

AFTER A HARD day's work it is pleasant to sit on the garden seat and observe how flower colours react to the fading light. Among the roses it is the dark colours that soonest merge into the gathering gloom, the murreys and the crimsons; the pinks and yellows stay visible longer; but the whites outlast them all. They are equally and uniquely telling in broad daylight, and no less valuable as a soothing contrast to all the bright colours of today. Among moderns we have the excellent 'Sally Holmes' and 'Winchester Cathedral' and the latest newcomer, 'Icecream', to act as a leavening to all the others. Since 1958 'Iceberg' has outshone them all and bids fair to last well into this new millennium.

History does not tell us when the first white garden rose was raised, thought to be *Rosa alba*, reputedly a hybrid between a white Dog Briar (*R. canina*) and a Damask rose, *R. damascena*, already a hybrid of *R. gallica*, which may well be considered as the grand-mother of all European roses. The so-called White Rose of York is *R. alba* 'Semi Plena', while its double sport, 'Maxima', is sometimes known as the Jacobite Rose.

Both make very large bushes and would be quite out of place in a conventional rose garden, assorting better with flowering shrubs. Another hybrid of *R. gallica*, called *R. centifolia* on account of its large, fully double flowers, has been immortalised by Dutch artists of the sixteenth and seventeenth centuries. It did not produce a white form until after the emergence of the pink Moss rose in 1727. The white form, *R.* 'Muscosa Alba', occurred as a sport in 1790, and was known as 'White Bath' or 'Shailer's White'.

Likewise the Damask rose, whose repeat-flowering form *R. damascena* 'Bifera' was cultivated in warm Alexandria and its flowers imported for Nero's feasts in Rome in autumn, produced a mossy-budded sport. This in turn gave rise to a white sport, *R. d.* 'Muscosa Alba'; it has not great quality and its 'moss' is harsh to the touch, but it is well-scented; it often sports back to the original pink. We still have two superb white Damask roses, the incomparable 'Madame Hardy' of 1832, and 'Madame Zoutmans' of four years later. The former has strong growth, good foliage and scent, while 'Madame Zoutmans' is of rather lax growth; but both produce their large, flat flowers packed with small petals only at midsummer. They represent the perfection of the old European roses, and have never been surpassed.

But this class of roses received a jolt around 1800, when four equally ancient roses reached Europe from China: two pinks (more than a thousand years old), one pale yellow tea-scented climber, and a true crimson, all repeat-flowering. These last two colours were new to Europe. Proper hybridising was not understood until late in the nineteenth century, but the bees did their bit and by degrees through the century the pale yellow gave rise to the Noisette roses and the crimson brought new rich colours to the Hybrid Perpetuals, of which the pure white 'Frau Karl Druschki' is still famous. It is a vigorous plant, a prolific repeat-flowerer, with superb scrolled blooms like those of the Hybrid Teas, but alas! no scent. It is intriguing to speculate what heights of popularity it might have achieved if it had been endowed with fragrance.

Meanwhile the Bourbon class of roses had arisen and has left us a very beautiful variety, 'Boule de Neige', of 1867; it is still grown, a good tall bushy plant in constant production of double, ivory white flowers of camellia-like perfection, deliciously fragrant. White has also survived in the Tea Rose class in the climber 'Madame de Sombreuil', raised in 1850, with the old style of flat flowers densely filled with small petals, and an unforgettable rich fragrance. It produces flowers throughout the growing season on a vigorous plant.

Delicate tea scent is also a noted character of 'Mrs Herbert Stevens', raised in 1910, with superlative long-petalled Hybrid Tea-style flowers in ivory white. Because unfortunately it nods its head, it has for long been passed by as a bush, but a climbing sport which occurred in 1932 is still grown with delight. Two large-flowered white Hybrid Teas, 'Madame Jules Bouche' (1900) and 'Marcia Stanhope' (1922), had their little reign, but are seldom seen today. In 1947 came the next landmark, the French-raised 'Virgo', which long held the premier position among large-flowered white roses until the coming of 'Sally Holmes'.

It may be as well to mention *R. rugosa* here, a pink rose brought to Europe from Japan in 1796. It has so many good points – vigorous growth, repeat flowering, large heps and healthy green foliage turning to bright yellow in autumn – yet it has never entered the mainstream of hybridisation. Nothing was done with it for almost a century, but it is a variable species, and two splendid whites appeared, the single 'Alba' and the double 'Blanc Double de Coubert', remarkable for their cold purity, along with some good pinks and crimson-purples. Rugosa roses do not thrive in very limy soils, preferring a sandy medium.

The little history so far attempted has been concerned with what we should call large-flowered roses, and there is another story, running concurrently, respecting the smaller-flowered ramblers. In 1827 a variety called 'Félicité Perpétue' was raised in France, reputedly between two European natives, *R. sempervirens* and *R. moschata*, both classes in a section of their own, the Synstylae. This name refers to the fact that the several central styles are united into a column; but more interesting and significant to us is that their sweet fragrance emanates from the stamens, not from the petals – so that the flowers of 'Félicité Perpétue', packed as they are with petals, have few stamens and little or no scent. It is a hardy old plant, still grown, but found more usually in its dwarf, repeat-flowering sport 'Little White Pet', of 1879.

The Musk rose, *R. moschata*, deserves separate mention. Although it is looked upon as a species, its provenance is not known with certainty – it appears as a native in many parts of southern Europe and western Asia; moreover, it sports to branches bearing double flowers. A semi-climber to about 12 feet or so, it does not flower before August, carrying on into the autumn, and like all the Synstylae species it is exceptionally fragrant. The flowers are creamy white, their petals rolled back at the edges. It might be thought that it would have made its mark among the older hybrid roses, but only two have come down to us which perpetuate the late-flowering habit, the little-known 'Princesse de Nassau', and 'Aimée Vibert' (1828). Like the type, neither produces flowers in early summer, but they go on flowering into the autumn. The first is a small grower with light green leaves and creamy, intensely fragrant flowers; the second is very vigorous with splendid dark green leaves, but the sprays of double blooms are not scented.

The Synstylae species are found around the northern hemisphere, with the greatest concentration between Nepal and China. Many are ramblers of great vigour, the largest being *R. filipes*, of which the specimen at Kiftsgate Court in Gloucestershire has achieved a height of 40 or so feet and a width of 100 feet – not a suitable species to cover an old apple tree, as is frequently recommended. Other magnificent, vigorous, scented ramblers of large size are *R. mulliganii*, *R. brunonii*, *R. multiflora*, *R. rubus* and *R. helenae*. Many seedlings have also been named, such as 'Bobbie James' and 'Lykkefund'. They flower at midsummer and their delicious fragrance pervades the whole garden. They have much to offer us, but I will not go further into them here; details can be found in my *Rose Book*. Other old sweet-scented ramblers still grown and loved are 'The Garland', 'Madame Plantier' and 'Madame d'Arblay', all raised in 1835. 'Sanders' White' dates from 1912 and is still the most popular white rambler of normal size. All owe their qualities to *R. multiflora* and *R. moschata*.

Those of you who live in warm climates may revel in two unique species which have not been used in general hybridising – *R. laevigata* and *R. bracteata*, both of which came from China in 1793. The latter was a parent of the famous 'Mermaid' but has white blooms, and flowers from late July onwards; it is perhaps not extravagant to claim that it is the most exquisite of all white roses. Its foliage is glossy, dark and all that could be desired, and its prickles are endearing too – they will let go! As to *R. laevigata*, it is a strong grower, so successful as a coloniser in Georgia, USA, that it has been adopted as the State flower, surely a recognition unparalleled.

Autumn

T HE AUTUMNAL EQUINOX falls on September 23, very often bringing blustery wind and rain that make us feel summer has gone. In Surrey there may even be a touch of frost. But all is not yet over, and October often heralds St Luke's Little Summer – a sweet, still spell of warm weather when our little treasure, the robin, starts to sing again. Spiders fatten, ready to deposit their eggs, bees set about gathering the last crop of honey and pollen, and wasps become drowsy from too much fruit, and cooler nights. The last of summer's flowers are spread before us, and it is the time for gathering apples and pears and carting them away to store, the apples in cool or even damp shelves and the pears in warm drawers. Harvest Festivals are offerings of thankfulness for the year's bounties.

The leaves start to fall in October. If you have time to spare and the air is warm enough, there are few pastimes so beguiling as watching one leaf after another, released from its parent branch, glide hesitantly to the ground, there to decompose and bring fertility for another season. By November there will be enough leaves to start sweeping. Lawns may be heavy with dew, and the conkers will be falling. Now is the time, while the soil is still warm, and (we hope) moist from recent rains, to move plants to fresh places, carrying out resolves made in summer days when sitting on the garden seat. November is the season, too, for bonfires – so long as you are not in a built-up area. There is joy for me in a whiff of bonfire smoke, which carries me back to childhood, when combustible material was stored ready for November 5, Guy Fawkes Day, with its attendant display of rockets and Roman candles.

As soon as the ground is really moist in November it is the season for tree and shrub planting. Shrub planting can go on until the spring, now that so many are grown by the nurseries in containers, but trees are another matter. Anything of a standard nature (that is, with a stem of a man's height) needs to be firm and established before the winds of March start to blow.

Winter can sometimes set in early, even before the end of November, and it is often claimed that an early spell of freezing weather indicates that the rest of the winter months will be mild; certainly this is what has happened of late years. Nevertheless, autumn remains a time of ripeness and fulfilment, and no autumn can go by without this thought.

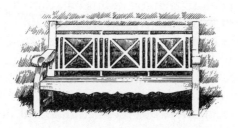

CHAPTER ELEVEN

The joys of autumn

'WHAT ARE THESE joys?' certain folk would ask, those who are only captivated by spring's youthful frolics and summer's abundance. But there are highlights for all of us in autumn, in the garden, in the orchard and in the fields. I refer especially to those wonderful days, in arable country, when the ploughshare has cut glossy furrows through the fields and the rooks and seagulls are wheeling and swooping after grubs and worms, lightening the air with their cries. And, down-wind, the smell of the turned earth refreshes us and makes us realise that a new cycle has started, not to be completed until the year has almost come full circle.

There is dew on the grass again, and on the cobwebs, catching the light, and the aroma from fallen leaves, at their most potent in the sharp smell of the walnut and the luscious strawberry-jam fragrance of the *Cercidiphyllum*. There is the glory of leaves turning to brilliance as a result of nature's cleverness in cutting off the sap just at the right moment; once the leaves have fallen there is that miracle of a view revealed that we have not seen since spring. The birds start to sing again, a gloating paean, perhaps in anticipation of the berries maturing on bush and tree. And gladly do we greet the smell of the earth when the autumnal equinox brings not only wind but rain – even though the rain puts an end to those flowers lingering bravely past their time – *Aster* × *frikartii*, for instance, the peerless white Japanese anemones, the nasturtiums and dahlias, the last outburst of roses from creamy 'Albéric Barbier', blushing 'Stanwell Perpetual' and the ancient yellow 'Desprez à fleur jaune', to say nothing of the moderns.

There is the weekly grooming to be done, the removal of faded flowers, a watchful eye to be kept on sow this-tles, which revel in the damp air, and the sweeping-up of leaves, which is almost a daily task, certainly in gardens where heathers are grown; they suffer more than any other dwarf shrubs from being smothered by wet leaves. Very often the wind which brings the leaves down helps us by piling them into heaps in corners. They look and are so bulky when gathered together that it is hard to believe how many thousands go to make just one bag of leafmould.

Autumn is also the season of many special flowers, so different from a few hundred years ago, when our floral delights in the garden would stop by midsummer, leaving nothing to excite us except the harvest and the crops of fruits and nuts. Having ransacked the corners of the world for late-flowering plants and shrubs, we can today glory in such treasures as that great shrub or small tree, the Chinese privet (*Ligustrum lucidum*), its lofty branches lit with pyramids of scented cream flowers. Nor is it the only shrub to wait till autumn to produce its annual beauty. The flowers of *Elaeagnus macrophylla* and *Osmanthus heterophyllus* may be small and insignificant but their fragrance compels attention as you pass by. *Olearia forsteri* is less hardy, but its flowers are no less delicious.

One cannot be certain of the flowering of *Viburnum farreri* (*V. fragrans*); in some years it is smothered with its pinky-white flowers in autumn, in others it waits for a mild moment in winter; but whenever it flowers, its scent travels right through the garden. The queens of autumn-flowering shrubs are undoubtedly the newer hybrid mahonias. Crosses between that old favourite *M. japonica*, with its magnificent foliage and comfortable shape, and the gawky, rather tender *M. lomariifolia* have resulted in several hybrids of great garden value, flowering bravely just when the days are reaching their shortest. Aloft they hold their sprays of yellow flowers for all to see – but though they have some fragrance they have lost much of the Lily-of-the-valley sweetness that belongs to the old *japonica*. They can make very large bushes, but seem to tolerate heavy pruning in spring with no bad effect on the following autumn's crop of flowers. 'Lionel Fortescue' is perhaps the nearest to the second parent, being rather tall and gaunt; I prefer 'Underway', which more nearly approximates the first parent in growth and colour; 'Charity', the first to be named, still takes a lot of beating; together they stand unrivalled among autumn-flowering evergreens.

The several years of summer droughts we have experienced in my area have made me appreciate still more what worthy shrubs are the camellias: they do not flag from dryness, as do those other charmers the rhododendrons. They mostly flower in spring, but I have a special penchant for the autumn-flowering *Camellia sasanqua*. Not well-known, it appreciates a warm sunny position to encourage its flowering. This species has not the impressive range of sizes and shapes of the spring-flowering *C. japonica* and others, but unlike them the flowers have a most delightful fragrance – at least in the paler varieties such as 'Narumigata', and the form with variegated leaves. It is unfortunate that 'Crimson King' has no scent: it is probably a hybrid.

We expect and are not disappointed by the coloured leaves of autumn. Theirs is the last great display of the garden round, before winter is upon us with nothing but berries and bark to cheer us. But I sometimes think we place too great a stress on the bright reds and flames. Where would they be without yellow leaves and coppery tints to give them contrast? A comparatively new shrub that gives palest green, ivory, yellow and pink as its leaves linger into the late months is that unexpected treasure *Cornus sanguinea* 'Winter Flame'. The wild species usually only turns to a reddish bronze at the best of times, but it is as if the bright clear scarlet of the twigs of 'Winter Flame', totally lacking any green or brown tinge, is echoed in the lack of chlorophyll in the leaves. And I may add that this autumn transformation is a long time in its unique enactment. It is unfortunate that it spreads rapidly by suckers, which must preclude it from all but very large gardens. Another shrub excelling in this valuable pale colour is *Orixa japonica*, which as a relative of the Rue family also regales us with a subtle oily perfume from its crushed leaves. I like to use these pale colours with reds which are nearer to crimson than scarlet – *Euonymus alatus*, for instance, and the delicate pinks of *E. verrucosus*. They blend well with the pink fruits of the Spindle bushes, various *Euonymus* species and hybrids headed by 'Red Cascade'.

Turning to the next section of the spectrum, there are the violet tones to consider, such as are found in the foliage and berries of *Callicarpa* species, of which the most noteworthy is *C. bodineri* 'Profusion'. From this it is but a step to the berries of true blue occurring in *Viburnum davidii* – you must plant one male with a group of berrying females – and *Symplocos paniculata*, which for some unknown reason the birds hasten to eat the moment they have turned colour; it is advisable and worthwhile to use black cotton among the twigs to frighten off marauders. Blue berries in their crimson calyces also swiftly follow the crop of fragrant white flowers on *Clerodendron fargesii* and *C. trichotomum.*

Outside the spectrum altogether are the puffy white berries of the snowberries (*Symhoricarpos*) and the dangling groups of white marble-like fruits on that gem among rowans, *Sorbus cashmiriana*, a tree for small gardens whose flowers are notable for lacking the offensive smell of most species and are pink into the bargain. Returning to our colour wheel, we must just have a look at some yellow berries before we come full circle to the scarlet ones. On *Viburnum opulus* 'Fructu Luteo' they hang in large bunches like glass beads, and in opaque yellow adorn *Cotoneaster frigidus* 'Fructu Luteo' – but this is a giant of a shrub, almost a tree; 'Exburyensis' and 'Rothschildianus' are hybrids of it with the more manageable *C. salicifolius,* and very lovely they are, too, with their graceful arching branches and pretty leaves.

There is no dearth of red berries. First among them are the cotoneasters, and I can think of few which last on through the winter so well as those of *C. horizontalis, C. simonii* and *C. conspicuus.* The first, so graphically described as the 'fishbone cotoneaster', presses its flat-branching sprays against soil or wall, thus displaying to perfection the multitudes of red berries. It is unfortunate that the variegated form, notable for its pink autumn colour, seldom if ever berries. Like them *C. simonii* is almost deciduous, and makes an admirable hedge; sometimes as late as spring its closely clipped mass will still show little points of red where berries nestle. As to *C. conspicuus*, this big, arching, sprawling shrub will already have caught the eye with its abundant white flowers in early summer; under the right conditions it will then be laden with scarlet through autumn and into winter. For charm and gracefulness I give pride of place to *C. salicifolius*, the willow-leafed cotoneaster. Few shrubs have a poise better calculated to display their bunches of red berries to advantage. With tiny foliage of a very dark green, *C. microphyllus* has crimson berries well-liked by birds. It can be used either as a sprawler, or trained up or down a wall.

I think there is no doubt that at the turn of the nineteenth century both cotoneasters and berberises did much to focus attention on all the many shrubs that were being introduced from the Far East, notably for autumn display. Berberises have somewhat fallen from favour owing to their excessive prickliness, but there are few more captivating sights in the waning year than species like *Berberis aggregata* and *B. wilsoniae*. Several hybrids have arisen in gardens between these two and other species and are known under expressive epithets such as 'Barbarossa', 'Sparkler' and 'Pirate King'; all have the great combination of leaves turning to bright colours just when the berries are assuming their coral-red tones. I challenge any keen gardener to pass them by without more than a glance; in fact, if you can get hold of the true dwarf *B. wilsoniae* (there are many lanky hybrids about), on a dewy morning you will be entranced by its colours, pale green and red leaves and coral-scarlet berries muted by 'bloom' making an unequalled picture for the time of the year. A shrub of greater size and heavier calibre is 'Rubrostilla', a hybrid raised long ago at Wisley, with berries shaped like a pear the wrong way up. And then, before I forget it, there is unique *B. dictyophylla* with an outstanding colour scheme all its own. The stems, prickles and leaf reverses are all covered with a waxy whiteness and the scarlet berries have something of the same 'frosting' over them. There is nothing like it, especially when seen revealing its most splendid effects against a yew hedge.

The flames of autumn are many. Who has not gloried in the scarlet of the turning leaves of those most lasting of all, *Eucryphia glutinosa* and *Photinia beauverdiana*? November is nearly over, but these two will carry on until overcome by frost. Of the maples there are scores from Japan, *Acer palmatum* in infinite variety and the no less splendid (though with fewer variations) *A. japonicum*. The autumn fires of *A. palmatum* 'Osaka Zuki' and its relatives – including the dainty Dissectum varieties – and *A. japonicum* 'Aconitifolium' are unbeatable. For their general wellbeing these maples prefer a sandy soil free from lime, and indeed it is generally considered that such conditions are the best to promote vivid colour.

The aronias never fail us in their brilliance, nor do the fothergillas. While *Aronia arbutifolia* is noted for its vivid red, *Fothergilla major* generally presents a medley of tints, red being predominant. These, and *Vaccinium corymbosum*, which goes out like a flame, are for lime-free soils, as are *Disanthus cercidifolius*, whose intense crimson colouring can scarcely be equalled, and *Enkianthus perulatus* and *Rhododendron quinquefolium*. I have often felt almost warmed by their vivid reds. Then there are accommodating shrubs such as *Ribes odoratum* and *Rosa virginiana*, which thrive anywhere. Of these two the former turns to red and orange very early, the latter to red later. And when contemplating shrubs for autumn colour, who could omit *Viburnum opulus*, the Guelder Rose? Though it gets very large in time it is worth every inch of space, rewarding us with white flowers in early summer, flaming foliage in October, and bunches of scarlet berries afterwards.

It is not only to shrubs we must look in our search for interest in autumn: some worthy plants flower legitimately at that time of the year. In a warm climate the lovely *Acidanthera murieliae*, now correctly known as *Gladiolus calliantha*, nods its white, hooded flowers with dark central markings, at the same time as the pink nerines, to which it makes a delightful contrast. The latter, *N. bowdenii* and its superior form 'Fenwick's Variety', flower best at the foot of a sunny wall. Their strap-shaped leaves last just long enough to make a setting for the flowers, then fade away until the following summer. With them I like to grow that astonishing daisy *Senecio pulcher*, whose strong magenta flowers do so much to enliven the darkening days. For the base of a very warm wall in a sheltered garden what better than that great pride of autumn, *Amaryllis belladonna*? Like the nerines it hails from South Africa, and from the ground thrusts up stout leafless purple stems to two feet or more bearing most gracious pink lily-flowers in a bunch at the top, of a clear and lovely tint when freshly open and becoming richer in colour as they age.

Chrysanthemums are a speciality of autumn, with the distinctive tang of the season. I am not one who grows great bevies of 'mops dipped in lobster sauce', as Farrer described them, but I have a fondness for the little pompon 'Anastasia' and its even smaller relative 'Mei-Kyo'; these are both of an indeterminate plum-colour, but buff and brown and yellow variants have recently come to light. I also have a liking for the so-called Korean varieties; but my special delight is 'Emperor of China'. I have been unable to find the origin of this, but there is an engraving of it in William Robinson's *The English Flower Garden* of 1893. Apart from the beauty of its subtle pink, quilled petals, its foliage at flowering time turns to dark red, and in fact it was this that enabled me to recognise it from old descriptions; I had grown it for many years without a name. I gave away roots, and it is now listed by several nurseries.

One of the last things of the late season is the Chinese Lantern, *Physalis franchetii*, an invasive romper, thriving anywhere and providing much colour for the approach of winter. This is excellent for cutting for the house, but should be defoliated and hung upside down for the stems to stiffen, to display the orange globes.

The crocuses and colchicums to which I called attention in Chapter 7 will have been flowering during October and November, together with the first snowdrop, *Galanthus reginae-olgae*. Forms of the Kaffir Lily or *Schizostylis coccinea* will be greeting us for a long time. I usually find that *S. coccinea* and its larger form 'Major', and 'Sunrise' in pink, are among the first to flower in late September, but they go on for weeks, with 'Viscountess Byng' to finish in November. By that month it is likely that some of the many forms of *Helleborus orientalis* will have been awoken by the cooling season to show off their cups of delight in white and cream, pink and darkest blood colour, spotted or unspotted, and the winter season will usher in the delicate creamy green bells in their branching spires of *H. foetidus*.

CHAPTER TWELVE

Paths

IN ANY GARDEN there comes a day, with the passing of summer and the onset of autumn rains, when the value of good, dry, firm paths becomes apparent. Paths are one of the essentials of the garden, whether to lead the eyes as well as the feet direct to objects of importance, or to stir the imagination by curving away towards a goal out of sight. Aesthetics apart, the selection of path material much depends on natural local resources. Cartage can affect the cost of a particular material; in some districts stone abounds, for example, in others it is a distant luxury. But the first thing to decide is to what use a path is to be put: is it for motorised transport, wheelbarrows, or merely footfalls? The answer will affect the choice of material. Normally some form of shingle or gravel is used. Today shingle is usually 'pea-shingle', crushed stones whose angularity tends to make them 'fly' when trampled, with an unfortunate effect on mowers if the path is next to a lawn. The shingle will also be picked up on one's boots if the soil of the borders is the least sticky. In the good old days real gravel, known as hoggin – a mixture of stones and sand of a binding quality – was used freely. The stones were rounded, uncrushed, and the whole was rolled to a good flat surface which stood wear and tear by boots and barrows. In frosty weather – and after – it might become sticky. One particular characteristic of old gravel paths is the gentle undulations. These were caused by the gravel being dumped along the path at regular intervals; it was then raked out to provide a flat surface, but never was the gravel so consolidated in the raked areas as it became, under its own weight, where the heaps had been.

On any soil that is not freely draining, but particularly on clay, it is necessary first to lay a foundation of clinker or coarse shingle, to ensure good drainage and dryness in all weathers. Then there are the edges to be considered. Bricks, tiles, slates, stones, even old beer bottles can be used for this. But if you edge your paths with old beer bottles, it does rather give the game away . . .

Because shingle rather than gravel is so very prevalent today, I think it wise to call attention to some of its disadvantages, quite apart from the danger to mowers (little stones have a fascination for small children, and I have seen them sprinkling path shingle onto lawn verges). There is also the discomfort and the noise of walking on a loose surface. The larger the screen – the size of the shingle – the less likelihood there is of it scattering. As to colour, I live in the Thames basin where all the shingle is of a yellowish colour, not always the best in a garden. The farther west and north we go the more likelihood there is of the local shingle being of a grey tint, so much more sympathetic to flower colours. In between, there occurs the softer, limy Cotswold shingle, not so prone to foot distribution and in various tones of creamy grey.

Even hoggin, when it is available, is nowadays frequently finished with a dense scattering of pea-shingle, but this brings with it all the discomforts and disadvantages already noted. If pea-shingle must be used, it is best to tar the foundation surface, then cover with the shingle and give a light rolling. This will deceive most people and be very serviceable, but where it is driven over, the little pebbles will soon loosen to reveal the tar. Another method is to mix cement with a naturally dry, sandy or stony soil, scatter densely with pea-shingle while still moist, and lightly roll.

Sometimes, where a continuous path is not needed, recourse can be made to stepping-stones. The best I ever saw were in A.T. Johnson's garden in Wales; they were home-made. A wooden framework about 20 inches square and 2 inches deep was made, the ground just covered with local grey shingle, and then the frame filled with concrete. When set the slabs were turned over for use with the shingle uppermost, providing a natural, anti-slip finish.

Bricks are probably the most-used of all paving materials, but they must be frost-proof and hard-wearing stocks. Old, second-hand ones give perhaps the best appearance, especially in what may be called gardeners' gardens, as opposed to architectural terraces. They are ideal for straight paths, but with curves their laying becomes rather involved; I think it is easiest and best to lay them lengthwise, following the curves. Elsewhere there is little limit to the patterns which may be achieved: herring-bone, basket-weave, fans, bricks flat and on edge, and many others. The effect can be varied by interplay with other materials such as stone slabs, cobbles, tiles and the like. Occasionally one sees paths made of crushed red brick of a soft nature; these look very well, but are apt to get terribly slippery in winter.

Where there is a lack of suitable local stone, or cost is a consideration, pre-cast concrete slabs are much used. Some are given a 'grain' in imitation of natural stone, but this looks as fussy when laid all in the same direction as it is upsetting when laid randomly. Plain surfaces are the best, of the sort of colour which will weather to the colour of the soil and not war with anything. I find 'crazy' paving upsetting to the eye also; it is cheaper to use slabs of any size and shape, but the effect is much less subdued when compared with random rectangular paving. The renowned Yorkstone paving has no equal, but its cost is almost prohibitive.

Whatever material is to be used, it is first necessary to see that the soil is properly consolidated; then 2 inches or so of concrete should be laid and the edging stones, bricks or tiles put in place. Then the next day the bricks or slabs, first wetted, should be laid on a freshly applied coating of cement and sand, wet and of a suitable consistency to hold the slabs or bricks and rise up between them as they are squeezed into position. This saves having to point the path, but before the cement and sand becomes too dry any bulging portions should be removed.

Salvation and reclamation are now fashionable, and an almost unlimited variety of materials suitable for paths is available from old builders' yards – hard dark blue bricks, red and other coloured bricks, stable paviours, road setts, cobbles; even roofing tiles can be used, if hand-made and with a sanded surface, but although they are highly attractive they will not take hard wear. All should be laid in the same way, except setts and cobbles, which are best and quickest laid in a dry mixture of cement and sand and then watered gently; brush off the next day.

All this hard surfacing presupposes careful thought about sudden thunderstorms and the consequent rush of water – perfectly all right provided the path slopes away from the house, but an encouragement to flooding if the slope is the other way.

A path or terrace, a paved sitting area or other such feature requires much thought, and a lot of hard work which cannot be described as gardening; but what enormous satisfaction there is in seeing one's efforts take shape, in exercising all one's capabilities to give the garden form and design. A path should lead from one point to another in a straight line, unless deflected by a tree or other immovable feature, or by the contours of the land. Curves gentle or decisive are welcome where appropriate, but never should a path be given a wriggle. Nothing is worse, except a double wriggle!

There is no doubt that on sloping ground steps can be an asset in terms of design and variety, even one step adding immeasurably to the interest and architecture of the garden; they can also be a nuisance, where wheeled traffic is envisaged. In a book which I had the honour of editing, called *Recreating the Period Garden* (Collins, London, 1984), Paul Edwards gave some illuminating details of what proportions of step to riser should be followed. He made it clear how important is the relationship between the height of the risers and the depth of the treads. I think we all know the discomfort of walking up or down steps of which the rise is too high or the tread is too shallow, or unnecessarily deep. Use specially hard bricks or stones for the steps; they take a lot of wear, and are exposed to frost. It is best to lay bricks on edge for this work. At Hidcote there is an interesting variation, in the use of tiles laid vertically, but they are comparatively soft and will not stand much wear. The wide variety of path and step design to be seen in old gardens would well repay some visits before completing plans for the laying-out of this very important asset to a garden.

CHAPTER THIRTEEN

Topiary in all its forms

FROM THE LATIN word *topiarius*, meaning ornamental or landscape gardener, stems our word
'topiary', which today refers to the making of artificial
shapes, either geometrical or fanciful, usually of evergreens. There is no doubt that formal, geometrical
shapes in sober evergreen can do much to quieten the
effect of some of our over-planted gardens, but in fact
they are best in gardens of formal design. Just the opposite effect is achieved when the topiary pieces are fanciful birds or animals; the whimsy adds a completely
different touch, and enriches the planting.

The most popular evergreens for topiary are Common
Yew (*Taxus baccata*) and Common Box (*Buxus sempervirens*). Yew is best for large shapes, on account of its
rigidity; Box is less self-reliant, and its branches are apt
to sag after a number of years. While it is possible to buy
ready-made pieces, the making of topiary from its earliest stages is a fascinating hobby. Where more than one
specimen is contemplated, it is vital to start with
uniform stock. Yews are generally raised from seeds,
with a consequent variation in growth; it is necessary

therefore that the plants shall match each other as nearly as possible in habit of growth and in foliage. Those with horizontal twigs are best; avoid plants of strongly upward growth. Box is as a rule raised from cuttings, but there are many types available even of Common Box, and it is therefore necessary to inspect the stock to secure matching specimens.

The ground intended for topiary pieces should be well dug and manured. Only when growing vigorously are young plants suitable for shaping; indeed, the growth of a plant some years old may suggest its eventual shape. Balls, cones and cubes require little imagination and expertise; it is when a spiral is contemplated, or a wayward plant suggests some arbitrary shape, that all our ingenuity is called for and supporting canes, stout wires and string come into play. It is wiser not to use wire for the actual tying of branches into place, for it may strangle a branch expanding with the years; the same applies to nylon string. When the eventual shape to be achieved has been decided, a stout cane should be used to secure the main branch – but I am going too fast: it is only when the plants are growing strongly, with shoots at least half as long as will be required later, that they should be persuaded to follow the line of canes, or stout wire; then, having got the main shape settled, superfluous branches can be removed, and we are nearly there. With cones, spheres and cubes the work is comparatively simple, and merely entails waiting until each specimen, growing strongly, has reached a suitable size to start clipping. Cones will usually need a central cane to guide the leading shoot. Sometimes the topiary is wanted on the top of a hedge: it is quite simple to let the top grow untrimmed for a year or more before clipping into knobs or finials. Much more elaborate framing and training is needed for fancy work such as fox and hounds, or a series of knobs.

This brings us to hedges; in fact, the very simplest form of topiary, but a huge subject we can only touch on here. The favourite for little hedges in knot gardens is the dwarf box, *Buxus sempervirens* 'Suffruticosa'. This can be kept to 6 to 9 inches for many years, and will stand reduction if it gets too large. Common Box is ideal for larger hedges, in which case the acquisition of matching plants is even more important than it is for topiary specimens. *Ligustrum ionandrum* is a box-like Privet which I have seen used for low hedges, and indeed for topiary, although it is not quite so reliably evergreen as Box. Yews are of course superb for larger hedges, also Common Holly, though here again there is the danger of seed-raising not always producing uniform stock. The broadleafed hybrid *Ilex* × *altaclarensis* 'Hodginsii' can hardly be beaten for a dense, dark hedge. It is a male plant and does not produce berries. A female of great worth but of rather lax habit is *I. aquifolium* 'J.C. van Tol'. *Chamaecyparis lawsoniana* 'Green Hedger' is the best of all the cypresses and thujas. Beech (*Fagus sylvatica*) and Hornbeam (*Carpinus betulus*) are both beautiful in spring and summer, and hold their leaves through the winter when used for hedging. The former is greedy-rooted, suffers from whitefly and will not rejuvenate from drastic reduction if it becomes too large, whereas Hornbeam will sprout from old wood. The many other good hedging shrubs include cotoneasters and berberises.

However closely clipped, all hedges gradually become larger, year by year. It is important to clip really closely, and the best month is August. Except possibly for bulky field hedges, never plant in what is known as a 'staggered' row, which merely results in a wide hedge – with added work in clipping the top – and no central line of stems to which to reduce the width if it becomes necessary. Since plants take in nourishment through their leaves as well as by the roots, it stands to reason that the clipping of a hedge deprives it of some nourishment, which should be made good by the application of a balanced fertiliser. This is a matter to be borne in mind with old hedges, and indeed all forms of topiary; equally important is the removal of weeds, ivy, etcetera from the base of old plants.

So far we have been concerned almost exclusively with ornamental evergreens – but topiary is also used in the kitchen garden, in shaping fruit trees and bushes, whether in simple fans or more elaborate shapes in cordons and other designs. The aim is either to grow the plants against walls or fences for added warmth to protect flowers and hasten the ripening of fruit, or, as in the case of horizontally-trained trees, to accentuate the design of the garden. All such artificially trained fruit trees should be grafted on dwarfing stock (raised from wild strains of crab apples in the case of apples, or Quince 'C' for pears). There are no really dwarfing stocks for peaches and plums, and the latter are not suitable for hard pruning. With apples and pears pruning is best done in August, to give time for flower buds to form. If one has the time and space, single or double cordons, even 5– or 6–stemmed cordons, can be readily achieved. It is a case of deciding upon the shape and arranging canes or stakes accordingly. In France, where the training of fruit trees is developed as a fine art, fancy shapes such as vases, goblets or pyramids are often favoured. These methods can also be applied to gooseberries and red currants.

Some keen gardeners also derive great satisfaction from a smartly trained pyracantha or other shrub attached to horizontal wires on a wall. There is much to be said for this method compared with the usual vertical training, and the results when in flower or berry can be arresting. There is no doubt that such training of trees and bushes lends much enjoyment to the art and craft of gardening. Achieving the sober lines of a topiary piece makes a complete contrast to other forms of gardening, and going round the garden with secateurs at the ready makes a wonderfully refreshing change from the destruction of weeds.

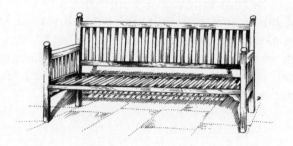

CHAPTER FOURTEEN

The value of lasting foliage

With the great gale we journey
That breathes from gardens thinned,
Borne in the drift of blossoms
Whose petals throng the wind;
Buoyed on the heaven-heard whisper
Of dancing leaflets whirled
From all the woods that autumn
Bereaves in all the world.

From 'The Merry Guide',
in *A Shropshire Lad* A.E. Housman (1860–1936)

WE DO WELL to remember that just as green is of
all colours the most sympathetic to our eyes, so in
the garden this same colour transcends all others. And
since you cannot have a garden without greenery, why
not give it priority in your thoughts? Foliage is with us
always, if evergreen, and for some six months if deciduous. It is not only life-blood to the plants but the whole
raison d'être of gardening. And think of the tints available! I have in mind here not the non-green colours, the
coppery tints and the variegation, but the infinite variety
to be found if we look at green itself: dark and light

greens, yellow-greens and blue-greens, silky grey-greens and glaucous tints, enough to inspire an artist for the whole year.

As providers of green, the most important are those plants whose leaves last longest in unsullied beauty. Any plant which holds its foliage in fresh array from spring till autumn is worth considering for an important position in the garden. The evergreen shrubs are worth their weight in gold – or nearly so! – and I need not elaborate here on the rhododendrons, camellias, *Fatsia*, viburnums, cotoneasters, laurels and many more. It is rather herbaceous plants that I have particularly in mind, and they deserve to be looked at in detail. A few obvious stalwarts are the bergenias, *Euphorbia robbiae*, and *Helleborus foetidus*. Some of the bergenias turn from their sober green to warm tints in the winter; the largest leaves among them, from 'Ballawley', become liver-coloured in cold weather. The species *B. purpurascens* is considerably smaller but the winter colour is an intense red-brown, a hue shared by the hybrid 'Abendglut'. Another hybrid, 'Morgenröte', has the added advantage of having a second flowering, in June. For sheltered gardens there is *B. ciliata*, with very large hairy leaves. There is thus a lot of variation to be found among the bergenias alone. The euphorbia and the hellebore, noted for the depth of dark green in their leaves, are totally hardy and evergreen. The former is an invasive runner, but long after the greenish flower heads are over the handsome new rosettes of leaves are in evidence, and last through till spring. Much the same may be said about the hellebore, but this native seeds itself only mildly and has black-green long-fingered leaves as a setting for its pale green bells in winter and earliest spring. All these plants will grow in any fertile soil in sun or shade. Similarly with the Japanese anemones: in good moist soils in sun or shade these regale us with handsomely lobed dark green foliage from early May until well after their exquisite flowers are over in early autumn – when, as a parting gesture, the leaves often gradually turn yellow.

I am very fond of the light green ground-hugging rosettes of leaves of *Campanula latiloba* 'Alba', and fancy that in this pure white form they are of a paler green than those of the normal lilac form. Although it reaches some 3 feet in flower, this Campanula should be placed near the front of the border for the sake of its long-lasting leaves. For sunny places the big clumps of foliage made by *Phlomis russeliana* take some beating. Its leaves are large, rounded and velvety-hairy, of a comparatively light green. Above the clumps ascend stiff stems bearing whorl after whorl of soft yellow nettle-flowers, and this early summer display is then rivalled by the seed heads for the rest of the season, even into autumn and winter.

While I cannot recommend for most purposes the great long leaves – up to 6 feet – of *Phormium tenax*, I think it right to call attention to this species for really large schemes in warm gardens. Fortunately *P. cookianum*, totally hardy, achieves only 3 feet or so, and its strong evergreen strap-shaped leaves are a splendid contrast to bergenias and other rounded blades. The greeny-yellow flowers are borne on side shoots up the stout stems in summer, but it is really as a foliage plant that we should value it. Nor is it generally realised what a fine foliage plant we have in *Iris pallida dalmatica*, and quite apart from its valuable grey-green foliage lasting from May to October, the flowers are lovely and fragrant in light lavender-blue.

For hot, dry, drought-stricken gardens there are all the larger sedums, headed by *S. spectabile*, with *S. maximum* and *S. telephium* as runners-up. Various hybrids are cropping up in gardens, among them 'Abbey

Dore' from Abbey Dore garden in Herefordshire, which has a fine sedum collection. They do not wake up until late spring, but remain in beauty until early autumn. The flowers may be pink (*spectabile*) or tones of plum-colour or dusky red. But it is their fleshy glaucous leaves for which the plants are mainly noticed. The compact-growing *S. spectabile* and its forms are a godsend for filling garden bowls and vases, since they scarcely ever need watering and look respectable from early summer until October. In addition to the glaucous sedums, there are several other plants of a grey hue – the trailing *Euphorbia myrsinites*, for instance, and that willing little glaucous *Hebe pinquifolia* 'Pagei'. This last is of course a dwarf shrub, but nevertheless well suited to the fronts of borders for its cool grey-green throughout the year.

Various pinks and carnations are also invaluable for a glaucous green effect in the fronts of borders – especially in well-drained limy soils. Such worthy varieties as 'White Ladies' and 'Cockenzie' are notably of grey hue, and a special word must be given to the old carnation which is correctly *Dianthus* 'Lord Chatham', but rather better-known under its more ordinary name of Old Salmon Clove. It was grown as long ago as 1780 and is still going strong, though it needs frequent renewal from cuttings (which are easy to strike). It does not flower until August, thus producing its richly coloured blooms – the tint of uncooked salmon – after most pinks are over. A glaucous note is struck, too, by that very hardy Poker, *Kniphofia caulescens*, whose flowers appear in early or late summer – according to the climate, I think; *K. northiae* has magnificent sprawling leaves, some 5 inches wide, of a glaucous green, but the flowers are not impressive.

There is nothing quite so grand, except among shrubs, as *Euphorbia characias* ssp. *wulfenii* – but perhaps I am wrong there, for it is semi-shrubby; each flowering stem takes two years to flower, like those of *Helleborus foetidus* and the noble *H. lividus corsicus*. The Spurge grows to 4 feet or so and the fine bottle-brushes of leaves begin to make their presence felt in early summer, just as the flowering stems are going over, lasting in spectacular array through autumn and winter until the spring comes round again. Then they nod and produce big heads of small greeny-yellow flowers, best in *wulfenii* and a few selected forms. As soon as these have passed their best, by July, you cut the whole flowered stem away – and welcome the new bottle-brushes in soft grey-green.

In sun or shade the dark green leaves of the Gladdon or Gladwin Iris, *I. foetidissima*, make a good setting for the pods of red berries in autumn and winter, but even in the form 'Citrina', which has the best berries, the rather dingy flowers are of little consequence. The beautiful variety 'Variegata' has leaves clearly striped with white, but I have rarely known it to flower.

Although I am only about half-way through my list of these handsome, useful plants, their wide variety is plain – and I have not mentioned anything new among them: most have been in our gardens for a hundred years or more. Allowed to speak for themselves, they create what today is called 'texture' in our gardens. It was Gertrude Jekyll who first woke up the gardening fraternity to the splendid qualities of such as bergenias, yuccas and Seakale. Before her influence on garden design and planting spread, the emphasis was on *flowers* for the herbaceous border, and as a consequence these borders lasted in beauty for only a few weeks, because it so happens that many of the most favoured border flowers have undistinguished foliage. Take, for instance, the erigerons, phloxes, heleniums, gaillardias and asters: their leaves are of little account, no more so than those of a privet. Weigh them against lupins, peonies, ferns and the other plants I am plying you with, and the contrast is obvious; moreover, the inclusion of good, lasting foliage will provide a feast for the eyes well into autumn, resulting in continuing interest of quite outstanding calibre.

Yuccas are upstanding plants with sword-like foliage, some of them shrubs, such as the most magnificent hardy species, *Y. recurvifolia*; others, like *Y. flaccida* in silvery green, are more or less herbaceous. The creamy bell-like flowers, borne in majestic spikes of some 3 to 4 feet, are one of the great glories of the summer garden. 'Vittorio Emmanuele' is a grand, handsome hybrid with reddish flecked buds, and 'Ivory' a shorter grower; both are free-flowering, and fragrant at dusk.

Among plants with long-lasting glaucous leaves Rue, in the good form known as *Ruta graveolens* 'Jackman's Blue', looks rather tawdry by spring; but for the rest of the year its filigree leaf-pattern is a great joy, specially when embroidered with dew or frost. I mentioned Seakale (*Crambe maritima*) earlier. There is no hardy glaucous-leafed plant of such overwhelming quality in its lobed and convoluted large leaves as this usual inhabitant of the kitchen garden. It prefers full sun and well-drained preferably limy soil, and spreads a bit by underground runners. There is nothing else like it in the hardy plant world, and it is worthy of the best place we can give it. The branching heads of small ivory flowers which it produces in early summer are a bonus, but I must confess that with me these usually find their way into a saucepan when in bud.

Having mentioned glaucous plants for sunny, well-drained positions, we might take a look at a few plants for shade. The most evergreen species among the many epimediums is *E. perralderianum*, with prettily tinted new foliage but in beauty through the year, making wide, slowly spreading tuffets of dense, lobed leaves as a setting for the airy flights of small lemon-yellow flowers which arise in spring. They occasionally seed themselves but are easy enough to divide, increasing yearly. Much slower is that gem for lime-free, humus-laden soil and part or full shade, *Galax urceolata*, which used to be called *G. aphylla*. It forms a clump of very beautiful, almost orbicular leaves of a shining dark green, deckle edged. In some years and where sun is not totally excluded, the leaves take on burnished or reddish tones. The whole plant, even with its dainty spires of tiny cream flowers in spring, seldom exceeds 18 inches. For a similar cool and shady corner is *Speirantha gardenii*, with handsome leaves like some glorified Lily-of-the-valley, but evergreen, and little sprays of elegant white flowers at the same time as *Galax*, in the spring.

Two rather coarser plants which prefer shade are the Lungwort and *Tellima grandiflora*. 'Grandiflora' is almost a misnomer, for the 2- to 3-foot stems bear minute creamy green fringed flowers, over handsome tuffets of hairy, lobed green leaves, richly mahogany-tinted in the form *T. g.* 'Rubra'. As to the Lungwort, I have already looked at their attributes and disadvantages in Chapter 1; they wake up the garden at snow-drop time, when apart from a few early bulbs, cyclamens and hellebores there are no herbaceous plants in flower, but their dull little flowers and hairy leaves begin to pall on the senses as the primroses appear.

Almost all ferns are long-lasting, from June until winter is spent. *Athyrium filix-femina* and *Matteuccia struthiopteris* are to be avoided for our purpose, however, since their short summer life has faded away by the end of August – though in moist climates the *Athyrium*, if cut over in that month, will produce a fresh and lovely crop of fronds for the autumn. There are several truly evergreen ferns, such as *Polypodium vulgare*, *Phyllitis scolopendrium*, *Polystichum munitum* and the blechnums (which, by the way, are intolerant of lime, though the others thrive on it). The polystichums generally, while I suppose they cannot be called truly evergreen, last well until winter arrives in all its fury.

Then there are some dwarf shrubs, such as the Cotton Lavender (Santolina) and the true Lavender, both of which blend with the flower border. If the Santolina is clipped over in spring goodly tuffets of feathery grey leaves will result, and we shall not be assailed by its acid-yellow button flowers, which can be upsetting in some colour schemes; *S. pinnata neapolitana* is perhaps the most effective in leaf. There is also a good plant with green feathery foliage and cream flowers, *S. rosmarinifolia* 'Primrose Gem'. The ordinary *S. chamaecyparissus* is not to be despised, either, even if it is left unpruned to startle us with its bright yellow buttons; it has a useful dwarf form, 'Nana'. As to the lavenders, if the flowering stalks are smartly removed from the bushes as summer passes, new little shoots of silvery grey will be produced which last through the season. The hybrid of *Lavandula lanata* called 'Richard Gray' is particularly silvery, as of course is the so-called Dutch Lavender known as 'Vera'. A newer plant is 'Sawyers', with extra bold flower spikes of a good colour. Unfortunately *Lavandula lanata* itself, with its very grey leaves and dark purple flowers, is not nearly so hardy as these others. I will conclude this little list with the 'Silver Carpet' form of *Stachys byzantina*, so long-lasting and so very silvery.

The choice is of course almost limitless when it comes to evergreen shrubs. There are the plain greens, the variegated, and those which assume new tints on the approach of cold weather. Among these last are

Mahonia 'Moseri', which changes to coral-red tones; certain forms of *Juniperus horizontalis*, which become violet; and *Thuja orientalis* 'Meldensis', which turns to feathery little bushes of plum-purple, even richer in 'Sanderi'. The genus *Rhododendron* alone would contribute to all these peculiarities – apart from variegation, thank goodness, although there are a few, a very few, even of these. Winter brings out the shining beetroot colour of *R. saluenense* forms, the glaucous effect of *R. calostrotum* and *R. lepidostylum,* and the copperbeech colouring of *R. ponticum* 'Foliis Purpureis', which is a desirable, compact plant.

With this medley of tints we must not forget true green, and here I find as the years pass by that few dwarf shrubs give me more satisfaction than *Hebe rakaiensis*, which used to be called *H. subalpina.* It is a dense little bush with small heads of tiny white flowers in summer and a brilliance of green foliage through the year, bright enough to vie with the best-kept lawn.

Winter

IF SPRING IS expectation, summer glory, and autumn a time of satisfaction, I think winter is a time of promise. In countries where the seasons are less marked, autumn and spring almost join together, but in England there is always a period which the pessimistic may call the dead months. If we accept that November belongs to autumn, December followed by January and February can be called winter; although, as I indicated in my paragraphs on spring, the early year is full of surprises.

There is something very special about December. It is the first time for many months that we are able to view the garden without the bulk of the year's leaves. Verdant lawns, sparkling with dew, take on a greater importance with long shadows slanting across them. In a cosy corner, where the watery sun strikes like a fading remnant of autumn, it may even be warm enough to rest on a seat briefly and watch the silent birds. The hollies are often full of berries – until blackbirds and the migrant fieldfares decide that the time has come to rob the trees of their crop. Two or three days are enough to complete the feast, with the result that our Christmas decorations will have to be made bright with artificial berries.

Seldom does a winter go by without at least a day or two when sparkling frost gives a silver edge to twigs and leaves, and if snow comes it brings a totally new aspect to the garden. The cypresses are bowed down, and conifers particularly need a touch of the besom broom to relieve them of the weight of snow which can easily spoil their symmetry. With a sickening thud the snow from the roof plunges down onto choice small shrubs by a sunny wall. But snow has its advantages, too; in dry districts its welcome moisture is released slowly as it melts, soaking into the ground beneath instead of running off, as will a summer shower. There is also the protection snow brings, blanketing tender plants against icy, drying winds.

We can garden in imagination in winter. Seated by the fire, if not on the garden seat, we can revel in the seedsmen's catalogues, deciding what annuals we want to grow, and where. Forking over proposed places on open days in winter will help to prepare a good tilth for spring sowing of hardy annuals, while on colder days the greenhouse demands attention, the cleaning-out of dead and decaying leaves and twigs.

Last but not least, are there not 'catkins on the hazel bough which speak to us of spring'?

CHAPTER FIFTEEN

Winter work

THERE IS A cult, observed by few it is true, which ordains that herbaceous plants should be left standing through the winter as a perch for hoar frost. While I am not denying the real beauty of some upstanding plants such as *Phlomis russeliana* when covered with that scintillating white embroidery, there are so many plants which autumn causes to bend down that I feel the lot are best cut away once the weather calls a halt to growth and greenery. The best and quickest tool to use is a sickle or 'hook'. Those unfamiliar with it may prefer a pair of secateurs, but this makes for a tedious job. Once all the deciduous plants have been cut down the remaining shrubs and plants take on a different set of values, and the late mahonias and precocious hellebores come properly into their own.

It is a time of assessment. The questions that will arise are concerned – if you garden for winter effect – with the value of the evergreen plants and shrubs. No bed or border that is seen from the house windows should be lacking in winter greenery, of value on its own, or because it is pricked out with berries or variegation.

Two very valuable cotoneasters which colour their berries in late autumn and winter and do not usually attract birds are *Cotoneaster glaucophyllus* var. *serotinus* and *C. lacteus*. The former is a very large bush which thrives particularly on chalk; the latter is a sombre evergreen of darkest calibre; both bear clusters of red berries. Among the newer cotoneasters is 'Gnom' ('Gnome'), one of the *salicifolia* breed with pretty narrow, pointed leaves. It can be trained on wall or fence, or used as a prostrate ground-cover for banks and slopes; the scarlet berries do not usually appeal to birds. They may take them if 'Gnom' is used as a ground-cover, but I fancy that the lax hanging branchlets do not provide firm perches. Certain pyracanthas also seem unattractive to birds; *P. atalantioides*, for instance, normally keeps its bright red berries well into the new year. Moreover, it is a stalwart upright grower with excellent foliage.

But evergreens with berries are not the only source of colour in the winter; there is variegation too. White and green are found in the lowly shrub *Euonymous fortunei* 'Emerald Gaiety', while 'Emerald 'n' Gold' is yellow-marked. Much larger is the splendid *Aucuba japonica* 'Crotonifolia' (if you can bear a large shrub with ultra-spotted leaves), and that best of elaeagnuses, *Elaeagnus* × *ebbingei* 'Gilt Edge' will both light the border and tone in with the Winter Aconite (*Eranthis hyemalis*) in January. For a total contrast, try the prostrate *Juniperus horizontalis* 'Douglasii', whose grey-green summer foliage turns to a violet carpet in winter. These and other low evergreens (see Chapter 13) will all help to furnish the garden in winter.

With gales likely in the early autumn and during the winter, it is advisable to examine all stakes and ties supporting young trees or holding branches in place on walls and fences. On sticky, clayey soils the movement of the necks of shrubs and trees due to gales is apt to wear a large wet hole which is very bad for the plants' well-being. In exceptionally windy sites an additional stake may sometimes be necessary, but stones or half bricks can be rammed in around the stake with advantage. On all young plants stabilisation of the roots is half the battle (sometimes the entire battle) in getting them to take hold of the soil, without which there is no chance of success. This is not only the case with newly planted specimens: it should be a follow-up precaution for a few years, until each plant is fully established and able to fend for itself. Old leather gloves and shoes provide excellent material for ties on wall or fence, held in place, loosely, to allow for expansion. These too need inspection from time to time, and tree-ties may need renewing. One of today's dangers is the use of plastic, nylon or other inorganic ties for labels. I have known them become so tight, from the expansion of the branch, as to act as a strangle-hold.

Then there is pruning, perhaps, to be done. Some trees develop a wayward lean, leading to a lop-sided effect or causing too much shade to be cast over certain plants; branches may need shortening, to restore the balance. Wall shrubs and climbers may also need attention. They are apt to be too vigorous, and clamber over less strong companions. The Winter Jasmine is to some extent pruned by cutting it for the house during the autumn and winter months, but a good chop back in spring will prove beneficial. The pruning of the various groups of *Clematis* varieties is well covered by catalogues and garden centre descriptive labels, but remember that the spring flowerers (*C. montana, C. alpina, C. macropetala* and their varieties) should only be pruned immediately after flowering. Roses are covered adequately in my own books.

It is sometimes forgotten that wisterias and certain

honeysuckles benefit from regular pruning. Wisterias need attention in early September if possible, but winter is not too late to cut away all the slender long trails that are not wanted for further training; remove them to the last few inches. These short shoots will, if pruned early enough, make buds for the spring flowers. Wisterias are usually neglected and become an untidy mass of long shoots, but by systematic pruning they can be kept to almost any size, as climbers or even as small standards. One very important result of such pruning is to encourage the production of short-branching spurs which will allow the flowers to hang free of the branches. Once a good stem has been achieved by tying it to a stake, honeysuckles of the native species (*Lonicera periclymenum*) and its forms 'Early Dutch' and 'Late Dutch', and my own namesake, together with the plant known as *L. americana*, will make effective standards, severely pruned to bring the bloom easily within reach of the nose. A series of *Wisteria* or *Lonicera* standards along a path will add wonderfully to the interest of a garden.

There are of course various regular garden chores to be carried out, if possible before Christmas. Leaf-raking is one, pricking the lawns is another. The latter cannot be done until all garden work for the winter is finished and traffic ceases; it is of great benefit, especially on retentive soils. All is then set for the new joys which burst upon us one by one at the beginning of the year.

With winter's extended evenings there is nothing left for us after a day's hard work in the garden but a restful chair by the fireside with a bundle of seed catalogues and visions of next year's plantings. Although my garden is filled to overflowing with good, permanent shrubs and plants, I like to find spots for a few annuals – old favourites which have been faithful friends through life and whose charms have never palled, despite a predilection in my old age for the more permanent garden stalwarts. I am thinking of such as the sweet-scented Alyssum (*Lobularia maritima*), whose hummocks of tiny white flowers add so much to the autumn garden; for some positions I like the 'Violet Queen' variant. The Night-scented Stock (*Matthiola bicornis*) is another old and desirable friend, for evening delight. Clarence Elliott described it as 'looking like nothing on earth by day but at night smelling like something from Heaven'. Just so. And who can live for a season without nasturtiums (*Tropaeolum*), so brightly fitting into bolder colour schemes? They are probably among the flowers of longest memory with most of us, with their intriguing, tasty leaves and gorgeous shapely flowers. These and others will all sow themselves year after year – not always in the right places, regrettably!

Then there are the biennials, plants which are easy to raise from seeds in a box or spare yard or so of ground, to be transplanted when big enough, and placed in their appropriate positions in early autumn. I have in mind Canterbury Bells (*Campanula media*); Honesty (*Lunaria annua*), best in the richly coloured 'Munstead Strain'; Forget-me-not (*Myosotis sylvatica*), of course; foxgloves (*Digitalis purpurea*), particularly the white; 'Miss Willmott's Ghost' or *Eryngium giganteum* (this should be sown *in situ* and not transplanted); *Smyrnium perfoliatum*, little-known but owing its popularity to its resemblance to the euphorbias; and of course the majestic, stately giant mulleins such as *Verbascum olympicum* which, when fully established, produces its great candelabras of small yellow flowers over a handsome tuffet of broad greyish foliage.

As to perennials, these are mostly increased from division or cuttings; primroses (*Primula vulgaris*), once established, will always be with us, though polyanthuses are not so trustworthy and need raising afresh every three or four years. For those on chalk or other limy soil the Cowslip (*Primula veris*) is a great boon and treasure.

Gardening is never finished, and the winter days are seldom long enough.

CHAPTER SIXTEEN

Lawns

WINTER IS A great testing time when it comes to garden design. In summer the garden is so full of growth and flowers that one is apt to forget how empty it will appear at the end of the year, and indeed in spring; such times will reveal how worthwhile is a lawn. That close-shaven greenery is the saving grace of many a winter garden, providing not only a foreground for borders but also a sort of canvas across which steal the shadows. Those of us who are lucky in having deciduous trees nearby will glory in the long, slowly-moving shadows of the short days. Winter very often also reveals that there is not enough light in the garden; when the branches are denuded of leaves, one realises the blessing of increased light.

If the borders have been cleared of herbaceous stems and mulched, perhaps, with fallen leaves, they too will present a flat array, this time of dark colour. Here and there are evergreen shrubs and plants, and it is on these that the garden relies for shape in winter. It is a good plan, when laying out a garden, to distribute the evergreen shrubs so that they accentuate the design, lending strength to the curve of a border or the crossing of a path.

With a new garden, it is important to get the lines of paths and grass and borders sorted out from the start. After marking the ground with pegs and string, one very valuable way of proceeding is to lay any permanent stone or brick paths, getting them just right. With lawns, things are a bit more complicated. Whether the grass is laid as turf or raised from seed, traffic – such as that involved in planting up the borders – has to be kept off while the grass establishes itself. One way of surmounting this difficulty is to incorporate in the design a flat stone edging to the borders. This can be laid before turfing or seeding takes place, and gives firm foot-fall for planting.

Almost any form of stone or composition material will serve equally well for this edging – stone, concrete slabs, or hard bricks (known as 'stocks') which will withstand frost; but if concrete slabs are used those with a smooth finish are best, of a tone which will speedily become muddied and dirtied and blend well with the soil. When laying out my own garden I was lucky enough to acquire some assorted pieces of Yorkstone. Their sizes and widths did not matter: so long as the edge fronting onto the future lawn made a continuous line it did not upset the scheme if some slabs projected farther into the border than others. They were laid straight onto the soil; in hindsight (and given more spare time), it would obviously have been better to have joined them with cement. This is because most lawns eventually contain some stoloniferous grasses, which tend to run in the interstices of whatever paving is used and so enter the border. If they invest such plants as pinks or thrifts, the consequences are unfortunate to say the least. Scale is an important matter for consideration. While in an average garden with borders of, say, 6 to 10 feet wide a line of paving up to 1 foot wide will suffice, for borders over 10 feet in width, or really large beds, paving 2 feet wide would not be excessive.

Levels must also be considered. If the grass is to be sown in spring, battens 1½ inches deep must be fixed to hold up the projected grass verge. A much easier way of achieving this most important initial matter is to acquire as many turves as are necessary to lay alongside the paving, to make an instant firm edge; for economy they can be cut lengthwise into two strips. The resulting turfed edge will indicate at once whether soil is needed to raise the intervening space for seed sowing, and how much. It is, all in all, a tricky job to get everything just right, for ground that is not properly firmed will tend to sink.

I do not think there is any finish to a garden so effective as this wedding of lawn and border by means of some sort of paving. It establishes immediately the correct line of the grass verge, and there is something very satisfying in the neatness of the verge and the paving invaded here and there by clumpy plants, which can flop forward prettily without causing trouble with the mower, and receive some protection from soil-splash.

Besides thrifts and pinks there are many plants which – solid, compact and, where possible, evergreen in growth – are specially suitable for softening the planting edges. *Waldsteinia ternata*, geums, heucheras, irises of the Pacific strains, *Viola cornuta*, *Origanum vulgare* 'Aureum' are just a few I have in sunny positions. For shade there are London Pride (*Saxifraga* × *urbium*) and its relatives, *Polypodium vulgare* and varieties, *Hedera helix* 'Little Diamond' and other ivies of a dwarf nature. They give an evergreen framework to the borders, a finish to the picture; they also tend to hold up the soil, and provide shelter for dwarf bulbs in early spring. To me there is nothing so winsome as this mixed edging assortment to usher in the fullness of the borders' later growth.

CHAPTER SEVENTEEN

The planting of avenues

IT HAS ALWAYS seemed to me that the fashion for making avenues must have originated in wooded countryside by the felling of trees to obtain long clear vistas, opening up the frightening forest. A clear way created through wooded countryside, visible from a mount or the battlements of a castle, was also a guard against intruders. Alternatively, perhaps they arose when a particular path was marked by large stakes which took root, as they would if willow were used. At all events, the making of avenues marking 'the way of approach' must surely have been concerned with either thinning or planting, according to the presence or absence of trees on the site.

These ideas merely call attention to the earlier historical perspective, before the laying-out of avenues became very much a part of man's desire to impress his personality on the countryside, particularly in the eighteenth century, when vast tracts of land became the playthings of wealthy landowners. William Kent was all for avenues; 'Capability' Brown eschewed them entirely; and Humphry Repton judged them to be right and proper, so long as they were not straight. He was responsible for a double avenue of lindens or limes, three miles long, at Clumber Park in Nottinghamshire, an exceptionally long avenue – even for those spacious days – which still gently pursues its way through the varying terrain. The idea of avenues radiating across the countryside, frequently crossing and recrossing one another so that endless vistas were opened up, originated in France. There they passed through forest and plough-land alike, enlarging enormously the already great formal gardens that were being created, and often providing a setting for *la chasse*, the hunt; Versailles is a splendid example.

Another factor was that in the eighteenth century a British nurseryman followed the inventive Dutch and found that the Linden or Lime could be reproduced in uniform quality by means of layering – that is, by bending down young shoots to the ground so that they take root. Nearly all very old avenues in Britain and France were by this means planted with the hybrid European Lime (*Tilia × europaea*), not only uniform in growth but capable of reaching a considerable height.

With the advent of smaller properties and grounds, grandiose scheming was abandoned. Shorter avenues were still planted, but very often they merely cut up the property, in a way that destroyed its entity; on the other hand, careful siting could make of them an asset, whether as a triumphal approach to a new dwelling, a windbreak along the side of a property, perhaps, or to screen neighbours' endeavours. Many short avenues of considerable age still exist.

In contemplating the planting of an avenue there are many things to be taken into consideration. First there is the terrain and the quality of the soil as a whole and, in particular – for an avenue is no respecter of nature's peculiarities – in the way of changes of subsoil, moisture and drainage. For more or less uniform growth, one must have uniform soil and drainage. I know several avenues which have been planted without due regard to these points, and with disastrous results, some trees (all of the one species or hybrid) growing twice as fast at one end of the avenue as at the other. There is no space here to go into the suitability of certain trees to certain soils – that must be left to other books. Let us content ourselves here with a general survey of possible species, and the dimensions of the avenue.

In spite of its unfortunate habit of producing basal growths (epicormic shoots from near ground level), the so-called European Lime remained a favourite with planters for some three centuries, probably because of that ease of propagation of uniform stock already noted. It has not I think been established whether this tree owed its popularity with the nurserymen to its prolific production of basal growths, or whether these basal growths were an outcome of its frequent use for layering. It has largely been superseded by the Red Twigged Lime (*Tilia platyphyllos*), but unless one goes to a true, natural stand of this species the seed is likely to be mixed. It is therefore often propagated vegetatively by grafting or budding onto stocks of *T.* × *europaea*, with disastrous results. However, the form *T.* × *europaea* 'Pallida' is nowadays looked upon with favour. The other lindens, *T. tomentosa*, *T. petiolaris* and *T. cordata*, would also make excellent avenues were they available in sufficient quantity.

Time was when Britain could show majestic avenues of English Elm (*Ulmus procera*), but since the devastating elm disease it has virtually disappeared from the land. As it was propagated by means of suckers, it is not without the bounds of possibility that all the hedgerow trees of their kind were related to one another through some ancient ancestor, hence their vulnerability to this disease. Equally splendid avenues can be made from beeches, whose great grey, smooth trunks and wide canopy of greenery are always inspiring. On no account plant an avenue of Copper Beech: in the mass its dark colour is oppressive, however much it may be admired as an individual specimen.

There are several oaks suitable for avenues, but like beeches they need their stems trimming from an early age, as they normally make low branches; trimming should be done when the side branches have reached a thickness of 2 to 3 inches. The English Oak (*Quercus robur*), a majestic tree, does best on deep rich soil; on poor soils, rocky, sandy or chalky, it is better to plant the Turkey Oak (*Q. cerris*); it is faster-growing and makes an equally impressive tree. There is also the splendid *Q. rubra*, a fast-growing, large-leafed American species with rich autumn colour, thriving on sandy soils. Its close relative, the Scarlet Oak (*Q. coccinea*), is also a native of the United States and resplendent in autumn colour; it makes a more tapering shape than the others.

One of the longest-lived trees is the Sweet or Spanish Chestnut (*Castanea sativa*). It can make a magnificent tree on sandy, lime-free soils, and in some conditions the attractive cream catkins borne in full summer yield a plentiful crop of edible nuts. The Horse Chestnut (*Aesculus hippocastanum*) is quick-growing but not so long lived. Its 'conkers' or nuts are inedible, and where they are likely to be a nuisance or hazard it is best to plant the double-flowered, sterile variant. One of the most beautiful sights of June is the Indian Chestnut (*Aesculus indica*) with its tapering spikes of pink flowers; avoid frosty hollows. The other pink chestnuts, *A. carnea* and *A. c.* 'Briotii', are not so fine.

I have never seen an avenue of willows, but can imagine that a fine effect would be achieved on moist meadows with the White Willow (*Salix alba*). It is a large and distinguished tree with silvery leaves and a luxuriant, somewhat drooping habit. I think we have better trees to choose than the Sycamore (*Acer pseudo-platanus*), but it has its uses, for it is tolerant of poor soils and wind, even from the sea. The Norway Maple (*A. platanoides*) is delightful in earliest spring when the bare branches are bespangled with bunches of yellowish flowers, and it excels in autumn colour; the Silver Maple (*A. saccharinum*) is likewise good in autumn, a quick-growing, graceful tree, with silvery grey undersurfaces to its leaves, but would require careful attention while young to achieve a well-shaped tree.

The London Plane, a hybrid (*Platanus* × *acerifolia*), is the largest-growing tree in southern Britain, achieving 120 feet, with a massive trunk. On most soils it is also long-lived, but achieves its greatest size with some moisture. Though the effect of an avenue of this tree can be seen in many a London square and road, I have yet to see one planted elsewhere, except at Windsor – surprisingly, because it is easily propagated from cuttings placed in the open ground in winter. Its splendid leaves are a fitting size for so large a tree. The same may be said of the Tulip Tree (*Liriodendron tulipifera*), another very noble tree, a native of eastern North America whose wood produces the American whitewood of the timber trade. It is one of the most imposing large trees and turns to brilliant yellow in the autumn. The unusual green and orange flowers appear in summer on long-established specimens, but are rather lost among the luxuriant leafage.

Also with large and imposing leaves, as discussed in Chapter 9, are the Indian Bean trees. Of the two most usually planted, *Catalpa speciosa* would be the more useful for an avenue because it is more erect-growing than *C. bignonioides*. Both flower best in the summer following a hot year. In Chapter 9 we also looked at a large-leafed North American Walnut; for an avenue we might rather consider the common Walnut (*Juglans regia*). It is a fine sight in winter but dull in spring and autumn, and its flowers are of no account. The same may be said of the Black Walnut (*J. nigra*) – whose fruits are virtually inedible – but its general growth and fine pinnate foliage redeem it. It can make a most imposing tree, but I do not know of an avenue devoted to it.

There are many fine avenues of Wellingtonias (*Sequoiadendron gigantea*); in spite of its California provenance it does well in most parts of the British Isles and grows rapidly on good soil when young. Nobody knows how tall it may grow; there are many specimens over 100 feet and some reaching 150 feet or more. There is no doubt that it is a highly imposing tree and eminently suitable for a grand formal avenue, but be sure to get seed-raised stock. Its rich plumose greenery is only equalled in beauty by its shaggy red-brown trunk.

Among conifers I think *Abies* and *Picea* would be best for avenues, but one seldom sees them so used. My favourite Scots Pine (*Pinus sylvestris*) might be used, if raised from a pure stand in Scotland, but normally its growth is too wayward for such a formal feature, although its pinkish brown bark in maturity and its grey-green needles place it high among ornamental conifers. The Redwood (*Sequoia sempervirens*), like the Wellingtonia a Californian, is not so hardy in these islands and frequently spoiled in a harsh winter. As to cedars, I have seen avenues of the Atlas Mountain and Lebanon species (*Cedrus atlantica* and *C. libani*), but to my mind they are too much individuals in their own right to be used in formal rows; the Indian Cedar, *C. deodara*, might perhaps be more suitable. But there is no doubt that we are so used to seeing all these as superb isolated specimens, near some great dwelling, that it is difficult to visualise them used formally. Similarly, its wide-spreading, graceful lower branches are so much part of the beauty of a Western Hemlock (*Tsuga heterophylla*) that one would trim it up to a tall stem only with regret. Indeed, I think all these great conifers strike a rather gloomy note in our northern light. We have, however, some good deciduous conifers to consider – larches (*Larix*) and the Maidenhair Tree (*Ginkgo biloba*). Both *Larix europaea* and *L. leptolepis* are particularly beautiful in their scented bright green foliage in spring, yellow in autumn, but the *Ginkgo* is a skinny specimen for many years and would not be my choice, despite its lovely yellow autumn colour. The latest arrival from the wild, the Dawn Redwood (*Metasequoia glyptostroboides*), is beautiful in spring and in autumn colour. Like the Wellingtonia its ultimate potential is unclear, but specimens planted on good deep soils are already forming splendid young trees.

I must leave you to study the soil requirements and possible heights of the various trees mentioned – in specialised books such as *Trees & Shrubs Hardy in the British Isles* by W.J. Bean and my own *Trees in the Landscape* – before making your choice for planting an avenue. There is much to be learnt in regard to climate, soil, water table and subsoil, speed of growth, height and spread before a choice can be safely made. The space available must also be considered. With trees which will achieve in many cases a height of 100 feet one must be prepared for considerable width, perhaps as much as 70 feet. And while it is all very well, and highly necessary, to consider the size of the trees at maturity, it must also be borne in mind that unless sufficient width is allowed for, as the trees grow their branches will obscure the view down the new avenue for many years. This consideration gives rise to a further corollary: if the avenue is extra-widely spaced, it may be considered that no trimming of the stems shall be done, and the result will be a wide ride with a V-shaped view. With closer planting of the rows, the stems will almost certainly need trimming, and a gothic arch effect will be achieved. Furthermore, no view along the avenue will accrue until the stems have reached a goodly height. While in the first instance wide-growing trees can be employed, something narrower or even fastigiate should be the choice in the second.

There is not only the width of the avenue itself to be considered, but also the distance apart of the trees in their rows. Usually, in our endeavour to make an effect within a lifetime, wide-growing trees will be planted unnecessarily closely, with a view to thinning them in due course, and it is important to visualise this thinning at the outset of planting. I have had experience of the necessity of thinning where a solution was difficult: should alternate trees be taken out, or should one remove two and leave one? The answer depends upon the choice of species: no blueprint can be made to fit each and every avenue.

Nor can or should one put an avenue down just any-where: it should lead from and to some objective, or curve intriguingly. One possible modern use occurs to me. In these days when it is economic to cram as many houses as possible into a given space, their approach roads tend to wriggle in every direction; I believe it would be a welcome relief to the dwellers in these houses to have some fine straight vista incorporated. The effect would be both sobering and triumphant, instead of involved, inward-looking and petty.

As very few of us today have estates of a size to accommodate lengthy avenues of large trees, we may only be able to think in terms of thorns, cherries, crabs or sorbuses. Even so, the design of the planting will lead the eye to whatever focal point is chosen, the converging lines of trees, however small, providing a special view not obtainable in any other way; when the avenue joins gates and house, it will lend the approach importance.

So there we have our avenue with the right tree, correctly spaced and growing for some two hundred years. What happens when the trees begin to fail? We must bear this stabilising thought in mind whenever we plant a tree of potentially great size. It is a problem that crops up every now and again over the centuries – I have met it more than once. There are several options. Avenues can be patched – not necessarily with the same species of tree, in which case the semblance of an avenue will be retained always, though the trees may be of odd sizes. More drastically, the avenue can be clear-felled and a new one planted in its place; this however has its inherent dangers, from impoverished soil and the possibility of honey fungus (*Armillaria*) occurring. I think the best solution is to find another site and start afresh, but this is seldom possible.

> Shadowy aisles of pillared trees
> Now my errant fancy please.
> Dim cathedral walks like these;
> Nave by numerous transepts crost,
> Each in his own long darkness lost.
>
> George Darley (1795–1846)

CHAPTER EIGHTEEN

Winter flowers

IN ALL THE many years that have passed since I became a student at the University Botanic Garden at Cambridge, nothing has dulled the impression the winter flowers in that garden made upon me. Although I had visited it often before going to work there, my walks were confined to spring and summer, and so it was all a delightful surprise to see one shrub after another coming into flower in winter. And not only were there shrubs to be seen in flower, but lowly plants as well. To me there is something miraculous in the flowers to be found during the shortest days of the year, braving the murk and showing us what nature can achieve without the aid of a glasshouse. Since those days I have always regarded the few winter-flowering shrubs and plants as an essential for any garden.

In our own garden at home, January saw the emergence of the Aconite (*Eranthis hyemalis*), Snowdrop, and of course the Winter Jasmine, *Jasminum nudiflorum* – an indication of possibilities, no more. My first January at the Botanic Garden proved a mild one, and never did horticulture so blossom upon a youngster as with the several plants and shrubs that reached their best that year. There was that frail flower of quivering delight, *Iris unguicularis* (we called it *I. stylosa*, then) in royal purple, lavender-blue or white. Nestling against the greenhouse walls in full sun they throve, covered with blooms during mild weather. By the end of the month they were joined by the bluey-white of *Scilla tubergeniana*, whose topmost flowers on the stalk open first. Then there was the perky small *Iris reticulata*, of sumptuous purple and with the scent of violets. One could extol other such 'early birds' among small plants – *Crocus imperati* and *C. tomasinianus*, for instance. The former was cossetted in frames, but the latter had seeded itself by the hundred along certain borders, earning its sobriquet of the 'prettiest weed in the garden'.

But let us return to the shrubs. Although after several tries I have failed to flower the Winter Sweet (*Chimonanthus praecox*) in my own acid-soil gardens, it prospers elsewhere, especially when growing strongly; Mrs Earle, in her *Pot-pourri from a Surrey Garden*, recommended feeding it richly. Its nodding, starry flowers of parchment colour with murrey centres exhale a fragrance unsurpassed during the entire garden year. They last well in water, and will scent a whole room, but the shrubby honeysuckles, *Lonicera fragrantissima* and *L. standishii*, also deliciously scented, drop as soon as they are brought indoors. Nevertheless, they are a great treat in the winter garden. I think the hybrid between the two, *L. × purpusii*, is the most free-flowering, its almost stemless, small creamy flowers studding the branches for several weeks.

One very large shrub in the botanic garden, *Garrya elliptica*, with rather dull evergreen leaves, would not have caught anyone's eye during the growing months, but imagine my surprise to find it hung lavishly with pale green catkins in late January! Although of subdued colouring and without fragrance, it takes a high place among winter shrubs. Today there are also some fine selections, such as 'James Roof' and the hybrid 'Glasnevin Wine'. I always feel rather sorry for Laurustinus (*Viburnum tinus*); it tries so hard, with good foliage, prolific flowerings of heads of white from ruddy buds, growing anywhere in sun or shade – but on mild damp days gives off an offensive smell, like many other viburnums: it is best to plant it well away from the house! One of the most beautiful forms is 'Gwenllian', with extra-pink buds which are often followed by blue berries. This is a fairly new kind, not known when I was young. At that time the Fragrant Guelder (*Viburnum farreri*, previously *V. fragrans*) was just becoming known, fresh from China. Its bunches of pink-white flowers are deliciously scented of Heliotrope, and over the years it has proved a reliable flowerer for autumn, winter and spring, according to the season.

Having read many books on gardening by the time I took the plunge into horticulture, I knew that rhododendrons abhorred our limy soil around Cambridge. Judge my surprise, therefore, when I found in that great garden a bed of peat planted with these shrubs and their near relatives – and of my greater surprise to find two in flower in January, *R. dauricum* and *R. parviflorum*. Both have small flowers of deep mauve-pink, and are very much in peril from the attentions of Jack Frost. They were followed in February by *R.* 'Praecox', a more reliable flowerer and a more vigorous bush, also in mauve-pink. All three have very aromatic foliage, and the last two are evergreen. My interest in all these delights was fostered by a fellow student, Tom Blythe, a nephew of G.N. Smith of Daisy Hill Nursery in Northern Ireland. We became close friends, and on occasional winter visits to his home he used to send me little boxes of winter and spring flowers from that lime-free soil and softer climate, which helped to whet my appetite. Since those days I have delved further into rhododendrons, and am convinced there is nothing to touch *R.* 'Nobleanum Venustum', whose fine trusses of deep pink flowers respond to the mild spells that occur in winter. Usually its first flowers open in November and continue to do so whenever the weather is suitable, until the final flush in March. It is thus doubly valuable, in escaping the occasional total devastation from frost which afflicts the others mentioned. But its foliage is not aromatic.

On the end of the greenhouse range grew *Clematis cirrhosa balearica*, a dainty-leaved evergreen which produces its scented creamy green bells from December onwards. I have since learnt that it is very vigorous; it has ascended and almost engulfed a tall holly in my garden, and as I write – in December – carries about a thousand flowers. New varieties appear on the market from time to time; one, very aptly known as 'Freckles', is spotted with rosy brown over a wide flower.

While the witch hazels (*Hamamelis*) prefer a soil that is not alkaline, they will grow well in neutral or slightly limy soils so long as they are generously planted and top-dressed with peat. *Hamamelis mollis* was established thus in the sticky limy soil at Cambridge, and grew well. I think its sweetly scented, spidery yellow flowers with their dark murrey eyes entranced me as much as anything during my first winter there. It is pretty well frost-proof, too, and its handsome rounded foliage turns to clear yellow towards the end of the year; the flowers, moreover, last well in water. Nowadays I should pass by the ordinary *H. mollis* and plant in preference the hybrid 'Pallida', whose flowers are of a brighter yellow, better able to counter winter's gloom. 'Pallida' makes a wide-spreading bush, but the newer variety 'Arnold Promise' is more upright, and flowers after 'Pallida' has gone over.

Fresh on my eyes likewise were Christmas Roses (*Helleborus niger*), which enjoyed the stiff limy soil of Cambridge but have never grown well for me in Surrey; with them, flowering in January, was the hybrid known in gardens as *H. atrorubens* and another we called 'Bowles' Yellow'. This grew around a bed of ephedras at Cambridge, a kind gift from E.A. Bowles, that wizard of a gardener at Enfield in Middlesex, who was a frequent visitor. *Mahonia bealei* was also in flower, primrose yellow blooms, Lily-of-the-valley scented, freely produced on its gaunt, prickly evergreen frame. Today we should grow in preference *M. japonica*, which makes a more pleasing shrub.

But there was more at Cambridge all those years ago than just the satisfaction of my hunger for winter-flowering plants. There was the discovery of a branch on *Sequoia sempervirens* with extra-broad, somewhat glaucous leaves; I took cuttings, and it has since become known as *S. s.* 'Prostrata', though many plants develop a leader and grow upwards well; there is one on the rock garden at Wisley. These are now very tall. There were the red-twigged dogwoods (*Cornus alba*) and their green counterpart (*C. stolonifera* 'Flaviramea'), and willows with orange-red bark (*Salix alba* 'Britzensis'). Among the conifers was a splendid specimen of *Pinus monophylla*, a species which I should like to see grown more often: its pairs of needles are fused into one, and are of a conspicuous glaucous tone. In that dry East Anglian climate *Juniperus deppeana* (*J. pachyphlaea*) grew well; it hails from dry parts of the United States and like the *Pinus* is seldom seen in British gardens. This is sad, because it makes a shrub or small tree also of striking glaucous tone. Conifers in their wide disparities were as a newly opened book to me. The great cedars and pines, which did so well in unlikely soil for most conifers, found an echo in my heart which has never gone. One which I have now, a young specimen of some twenty-five years of age and about 3 feet high and wide, was a graft off a plant on the old rock garden (today the Terrace Garden), now about a hundred years old, and some 10 feet by 10. In my days at Cambridge it was called *Pinus laricio* 'Pygmaea', but is now *P. sylvestris* 'Moseri'. Here in my garden I have also that lovely *Mahonia* 'Moseri' whose foliage is coral-red in winter, and on the wall nearby is *Clematis* 'Nelly Moser'; all commemorate the famous firm of MM Moser of Versailles, France. The pine is dark lustrous green in summer, but with the approach of winter turns a bronzy yellow. Could one ask for more?

These glories of winter can all be yours with a little forethought, and I venture to prophesy you will not regret adding them to your garden plants. And to think that not one was available to gardeners in this country a few hundred years ago!

Envoi

. . . the garden-maker is striving not for himself alone but for those who come after, for the unborn children who shall play on the flowery lawns and chase each other through the alleys, filling their laps with treasure of never-fading roses, weaving amidst the flowers and the sunshine dream-garlands of golden years. They too will know bare winter's hidden hoard, when the earth under their feet is full of dreams . . . the rising murmur of insect delight, the scent of the sun-kissed grasses . . . the riot and rapture of spring, and the passion of the flaming roses, and that strange thrill of autumn sadness when the flowers that have mingled their perfumes through the summer are breathing out to each other the grief of a last farewell.

From *On the Making of Gardens*
by Sir George Sitwell (1949)

They will come again, the leaf and the flower, to arise
From squalor of rottenness into the old splendour,
And magical scents to a wondering memory bring;
The same glory, to shine upon different eyes,
Earth cares for her own ruins, naught for ours,
Nothing is certain, only the certain spring.

Laurence Binyon (1869–1943)

Location of seats

page

18 A pair of gothic-style chairs, of metal, in John Fowler's garden, Hampshire

21 An art-deco seat at Scotney Castle, Kent; natural wood finish

27 At Culzean, Strathclyde, Scotland, naturally shaped chairs and table, just right for a children's party

34 A magnificent seat made to fit a niche of Yew

37 A seat of unique design at Anglesey Abbey, Cambridgeshire

44 A seat specially constructed to surround a tree, with thatched shelter above, at Old Warden, Bedfordshire

47 A moveable seat in the conservatory, Wallington Hall, Northumberland

54 An elaborate Chinese-style seat at Wallington Hall, Northumberland

60 A rustic seat at the Savill Garden, Windsor

68 A seat of unique design at Heveningham Hall, Suffolk

74 A seat of traditional design at Hardwick Hall, Derbyshire

90 Traditional seat design at Sizergh Castle, Cumbria, made to fit the corner of the castle

96 A stone seat with paved surround at Knightshayes Court, Devon

99 A highly decorative seat at Heveningham Hall, Suffolk

108   A rather grand seat at Powis Castle, North Wales
113   Dry footfall and dry seat at Ickworth, Suffolk
118   A garden seat of a design fairly common in the early
       years of this century, at Chartwell, Kent
128   The castors and handles enable this seat to be moved
       about easily. The back is solid and keeps the seat dry
       when closed over it. At Powis Castle, North Wales
131   An elaborate iron seat at Powerscourt, Ireland. Black
       paint is well contrasted by the pale shingle, though the
       splendid metal-work design could well support a light
       colour
137   Rustic table and seat at Scone Palace. The seat is
       prepared and varnished, the back-rest likewise, and is so
       made that it can be folded over the seat to keep it dry
140   A strong, elegant seat at Plas Newydd, Anglesey
149   A metal seat newly constructed to an old pattern, at
       Arlington Court, Somerset
155   A charming seat in a Berkshire garden

endpapers
A   A simple bench at Shugborough Hall, Staffordshire
B   A fairly commonplace wooden seat at Acorn Bank,
     Cumbria, made inconspicuous by being stained and oiled
C   An uncomfortable seat, though elegant, at Clevedon Court,
     Avon
D   A comfortable metal seat in the conservatory, Wallington
     Hall, Northumberland
E   A wooden seat specially constructed around a tree trunk at
     Chelwood Vachery, East Sussex. Note the deeply 'dished'
     seat, aimed at comfort
F   A metal seat at Ickworth, Suffolk
G   One of several seats which could be fitted round a large
     tree bole. At St John's Jerusalem, Kent
H   This seat was carved out of a trunk of Sweet Chestnut at
     the Savill Garden, Windsor, supported on brick plinths.
     Drainage holes have been made at the back of the seat
I   An elaborate Chinese-style seat at Abbot's Ripton,
     Cambridgeshire

A

B

C

D

E